SHARING THIS DELICATE BREAD:

Selections from Sheila-Na-Gig online 2016-2021

Edited by Barbara Sabol

ISBN: 979-8-9855242-6-0
Library of Congress Control Number: 2022941358

Sheila-Na-Gig Editions
Russell, KY
Hayley Mitchell Haugen, Editor
www.sheilanagigblog.com

Preface

Perhaps the world will end at the kitchen table, while we are laughing
and crying, eating of the last sweet bite —Joy Harjo

It has been my honor and delight to gather poems from the first five years of *Sheila-Na-Gig online* into this anthology. The selected poems from the years 2016-2021 are by seasoned writers whose work most often graced the journal. These are poems that illustrate the journal's aesthetic: "excellent imagery and a strong sense of voice." True of the individual poems and even more strikingly so gathered into a collection.

Through these pages, the broad swath of relationships that bind us to family, to lovers, to childhood memories, to the natural world, and to our wounded society are enacted through distinctive imagery and voice. The reader is invited to delve into a profound truth: "the world is just as beautiful as it's hurt" ("Crivelli's Madonna and Child," George Franklin). Taken together, the work highlights the vital role of poetry to affirm our shared, keenly lived experiences as we come together at a common table to share the "delicate bread" signified in Seth Jani's beautiful poem, "Repast."

When I set out to pull these 107 poems together thematically, I found that they naturally fell into a seemingly preordained order, with a dovetailing of subject poem to poem, section to section. A true mark of the realized aesthetic this community of poets brings to the table lies in how the poets' singular styles blend so seamlessly into a unified voice. The pieces demonstrate how every shade of emotion hinges on a kind of delicacy: the core vulnerability that shapes our response to the world, and that connects us all.

I am grateful to Hayley Mitchell Haugen, *Sheila-Na-Gig* founder and editor, for entrusting me with this lyric treasure trove, and for her support throughout the process of creating the collection. It has been a joy to mine the first twenty volumes for the fine work contained in these pages, and to rediscover and savor the delicacies the poems offer, down to "the last sweet bite."

Barbara Sabol
Associate Editor, *Sheila-Na-Gig online*

Introduction

Sheila-Na-Gig, the Los Angeles-based print journal, launched in 1990, when I was finishing up my undergraduate degree in creative writing at California State University, Long Beach. Over the next ten years, including my time in the MFA program in poetry at the University of Washington, I went on to publish fourteen volumes of the journal and three chapbooks.

In 2001, I moved to Athens, Ohio, to pursue a Ph.D. in American Literature at Ohio University. At that time, I found it necessary to put the journal to bed as I pursued these studies. Flash forward fifteen years: I had completed my Ph.D., found a full-time teaching job, become a mother (twice), and made tenure. But I felt empty. Something was missing: poetry. My focus elsewhere, I had written very few poems during these years, and I certainly hadn't sent any out for publication. And while I wasn't writing or submitting my work, the poetry world had changed unbeknownst to me. It had become broader, richer, and more accessible. One no longer had to spend hours in the library with the latest fat edition of *The Poets' Market* to find suitable journals for one's work. Indeed, when a student introduced me to Duotrope, and I next discovered Submittable, I realized the full extent of what I had been missing.

I began culling through my old poetry files, sending out individual poems, and putting together the two collections of MFA and earlier poems that eventually became *What the Grimm Girl Looks Forward To* (Finishing Line Press, 2016) and *Light & Shadow, Shadow & Light* (Main Street Rag, 2018). Getting published is always exciting, but still, something was missing: editorial work. From *Sheila-Na-Gig*, to the *Seattle Review*, to *Hotel Amerika, Quarter After Eight*, and *The New Ohio Review*, my hands had always contributed to stirring that great big pot of submissions.

And so . . . in 2016, not knowing the first thing about how to run a website (beyond a very brief stint as a blogger), I sent out the first calls for submission for *Sheila-Na-Gig online* and received work that, quite frankly, blew me away. It didn't take long for word of my new/old journal to spread, and I was surprised at how many 1990s contributors found me and reconnected. One of these poets was Marc Swan in 2017. Having a few issues under my belt at that time, and inspired by the huge volume of poetry manuscript contests I had seen online, I was considering running a contest, but I didn't want to do so without first producing a book title. I asked Marc to be my guinea pig, and we created *today can take your breath away*. Thus, Sheila-Na-Gig Editions was born.

Since 2016, I have published over nine hundred poets (including multiple poems from our many frequent contributors) in twenty-four volumes of *Sheila-Na-Gig online*, awarding them $2,400 in contest and editor's prizes. I have published four anthologies (not including this one) and collections by thirteen individual authors, awarding over $9,000 in manuscript contest awards and royalties. It has been my absolute joy to support these authors' works, and even more so, to become friends with such a fine community of poets across the nation and beyond. One of these friends is Barbara Sabol who I did not know before she won one of my manuscript contests, and I subsequently published her book, *Imagine A Town*. Knowing that I had been feeling overwhelmed with an increased volume in submissions, Barbara volunteered to serve as a reader for *Sheila-Na-Gig online*. Her help has been tremendous, but she wanted to do more! When she told me she wanted intern experience on a larger project, I already had this anthology in mind. This project would have stayed on the back burner for years, however, had Barbara not been there to embrace it. To help her rein in the sheer volume of material, I suggested that she focus on authors who had contributed to at least three volumes of the journal. She has guided the project from there, reading multiple volumes, selecting poems, and ordering them into this fine collection. Thank you, Barbara, for the generosity of your time and friendship. And thank *you*—whether you be a contributor or reader—for helping to sustain *Sheila-Na-Gig online* and Sheila-Na-Gig Editions.

Nothing is missing. I feel complete.

Hayley Mitchell Haugen
Russell, KY, 2022

CONTENTS

"

In the window of a store
on a street we loved
where faces stopped to listen

—Daniel Edward Moore,
"At the Corner of Heavy and Acquaintance"

Devon Balwit

One-Half Specter

And for entertainment, a black scarecrow
No one ever bothered to take down —
a figure one-half specter and one-half clown
                    ——Brad Leithauser

Here in the aftermath, harvest done,
stalks rasp, bowed by crow shadow.

The fields fold in on themselves,
a corrugation of frost and wind.

I fold, too, hiding from the house,
its static of undone tasks. Balky

in harness, I refuse to tidy, to care
for, wanting just to hang my head.

Soon mother will clatter the hung tin,
a din she knows reaches wherever

feet can take me. I will home
to the flare of the sinking sun,

flickering as I light the stove,
hands blind about their business.

Rebecca Brock

Expanse, Immensity, Collapse

When did time start? my son asks, looming at 4 am.
The animal in me startles, cries out—
his face so close and sudden in the dark,
it's only a moment that I don't know him.
But it's the kind of thing he asks.
He could mean the tick of the clock,
his knowledge of bedtime, time to wake up,
or he could mean his own beginning.
Burdened with a restless mother,
he understands distance is a thing to measure
(how much longer mama?)
between here and there and when
we are on our way toward home again.
Already he's unearthed stories of stone fish
in a Wyoming desert, of cliffs in Nova Scotia
scored with prehistoric trees, an Oreodont skull
in South Dakota—he knows that rocks themselves have ages.
He might have been asking about old human things:
temple gods and sacred rites, lost cities—
he's raced his brother around ancient mounds in Ohio,
walked undulations of an earthen serpent's
twists and turns once aligned with moon, sun,
and steady seeming stars.
Do you hear that? he asks after I've coaxed him
back beneath the covers, snuggled down
beside him—a sound like clanging pipes,
like a radiator we don't have, shudders
and I rise to look out the window,
turn to tell him it is only hard rain.
There are at least two ways
to measure a life: the human one,
and the universe's grander score
of expanse, immensity, collapse.
I lie awake to the wash of it.

Kathleen Burgess

I'm a pilgrim light needles into place

No art is possible without a dance with death.
   —Kurt Vonnegut, *Slaughterhouse Five*

Stitches drop from a quilted sky.
        Light fractures. No. That was then.

Now skeins of cirrus
        reflect the cold ordinary.

I'm about to pack away
        ornaments of the old year.

Under January's ceiling,
        green branches jangle icicles, bells.

The glass rings a mantra,
        a summons unraveling time.

I've seen Time slow,
        as one arthritic hand casts on.

Knit forward. Purl back. Bind off, clip,
        and done. Buttoned up but crooked.

One moment I'm walking upstairs;
        the next, blinded by sun-flash

through window glass—
        the way klieg lights usher

a hero into the Hall of Death,
        through a bright, illusory doorway.

Into a silence dreamt backwards,
          ice sweaters a freeway bridge.

The car's a slow-motion accordion
          squeezed by an ambulance.

In the back seat children wake in terror.
          We rub our eyes. Glitter for days.

Jennifer Hambrick

Seed

There is no child I can teach this to –

troweling slits in dirt,
dropping sunflower seeds,

with a stoic prayer I guard against
disappointment from still, cold

ground, settling to hope for not
the feeling it might bring, but

just the thing. Seeds crack
the flesh that feeds them,

oblong leaves on spindly stems
unwind into air and space

they know they do not have
to earn. They'll grow tall

if other creatures don't
destroy them. Every child

needs to learn that sowing
doesn't always lead to reaping.

Inside this house are doors
we do not open. Windows ache

with the grime of silent years.
In waking hours my fist uncurls, anxious

of what might drop into its palm,
the heavy hollow pit it has to carry.

Stan Savel Rubin

Max's Garage
for my grandfather

i.
His leather thumbs popped metal caps from bottles
yet his hands did the work of precision,

carefully opening the possibilities of wood
to take a shape we desire

despite wood's hardness, despite
the tendency of all things to resist us

the way his tools resisted me,
my clumsy touch.

Nevertheless, he gifted me with hammers, chisels,
saws I looked at fearfully like sharks in a story.

ii.
He tried to teach me
how tape measure and T-square can make shapes true,

how the green liquid trapped in the eye of the level
is a prophet of certainty,

if one can only learn to read it right,
the way he did.

iii.
He said little, knowing little
of my language,

bookish American schoolboy
who dreamed of being a sports star yet couldn't see the difference

a sixteenth or thirty-second makes in everything.
He grunted approval when things worked,

grunted disapproval when they didn't and went on.
A craftsman never accepts imperfection as final.

iv.
Standing next to him in the noisy garage,
reeking of cigarettes that finally killed him,

I covered my ears when the table saw growled
and he pushed me back from the threat of the blade.

John Palen

The Back Shop

Deep in the back of the building,
far from Uncle Bud's genteel office
with its revises and flimsies,
Uncle Pete had his domain,
hot as a foundry, busy as hell.
Wheeled iron turtles,
chases, quoins and a hellbox.
The Linotype's metallic clatter,
smells of gasoline and cigarettes,
oil and grit on every surface,
a thinning oval of Lava soap
on a basin stained with ink and rust.

He sends me to the alley for lead pigs,
two-foot gray bars in a pile
among tall dandelions.
I get a penny each to bring them in.
From a hooked chain they'll feed
a lead pot at 700 Fahrenheit,
hot enough to explode
if he spills his Coke.

Deadline nears.
His quick two-fingered jabs
add weight to words,
casting them into type.

Kari Gunter-Seymour

Trigger Warning

November is the month my son dreads.
Too many dead in November, he says.
When they come to him now, it's as
full body experiences, rapid-fire,
built of muscle memory, bile in his mouth,
propellant fumes, exit wounds, zippered bags.
I cradled them, until
there was just nothing there.

My only frame of reference,
the way my father fought for last breaths,
shook, straightened his crippled legs.
Or every dear old dog, I rocked
on my heels, eyes to the sky,
knowing it was their time.

Outside my window, two deer
are shadow shapes, hides dappled
by light as they forage for acorns,
capped confections, hidden
beneath tapestries of coppered leaves.
A red-tailed competes for my ears.

What I am afraid of, is never finding
the brave heart my son had been,
the farm boy, the quipster,
the Ren & Stimpy impersonator
who boarded the plane, now camouflaged
in anxiety meds and a skeletal body.

A blue jay pecks a seedcake,
a sparrow picks at crumbs below.

Two cardinals, one perched,
one wing-fluttering at the feeder,
vie for millet, their feathers edged
in morning sun.

When my father visits me in memory,
he often saunters through my head
the way he sauntered through my childhood,
pausing to light a Parliament Menthol,
reminding me to not take shit from anyone,
but always own up to my mistakes.

We don't get to choose our memories,
they are triggered.
Guilt comes the same way,
unreeling from our darkest places,
the awful wait for the agonal breath.

Alan Walowitz

Sundown

Though she was known to nap after breakfast,
my mom would wake in time to see me
sitting in the wing chair, and demand,
Where did you fly in from?
Superman, I'd say–
I came through the window.
And she'd laugh that half-bitter laugh
I knew by heart, having learned at her knee.
She'd reach for the coffee I brought, one hand shaking
and try to steady it with the other,
pick at the obligatory sweet roll and nod off again.
Alma, her aide, would say to me then,
Wise guy. Why you so early?
Come later when she's mean and pinches me.
My mother would never, I tell her.
Come 4 o'clock. You'll see—
and she shows me the red mark
on her arm from yesterday.
I avert my eyes and go to the window
where I flew in, and assure everyone–
even those who have nodded off again–
I'll fly back in the morning to see.

Carol Lynn Stevenson Grellas

Because It's Easy to be Sad about Anything

My mother always said she liked the nakedness
of bare feet the vulnerability of her sole

walking across grass. The idea of shoes
waiting empty and unused in a closet.

But after she died, I saved her favorite heels,
stuck them in a laundry room drawer

and forgot they were there, until I was
searching for something I'd lost. And

I'm sorry now, that I didn't bury her
in those shoes, that I found them while

looking for a mislaid thing, which made me
miss her even more, which made me see

her shoes a little differently, as if they were
there to remind me that she was off somewhere

without me, without her favorite shoes,
walking alone, walking barefoot

across grass.

Louisa Muniz

Stone Turned Sand

I kiss the orchid petals
on the kitchen counter.

Whisper a secret into the plant.
I kiss a picture of my sons.
My framed world.

I once carried a fetus
for ten weeks four days two hours.
Prayed for a girl.

I carried her: Fabergé egg
of guilloché enamel.
Body dawning song.

I touch the lip of the orchid,
a landing platform for insects,
attracted to the curved shape.

Look how the light glints
through the drapes,
ornaments the tiled floor.

I am a quiet plea of honey bee.
Each weight-bearing wing
carrying stone turned sand.

Rebecca Dettorre

Fort Steuben Bridge

Nineteen-seventy-four, it rained
all summer. At least that's
what I remember. I was eleven.
Each week our father piloted
a Buick with the family, all seven,
across state lines for Sunday
dinner, the towns divided
by a river. Each week,
I noted the water rise,
treetops gradually submerged
on steep banks, imagining
the Ohio reaching asphalt
on both sides of rusted
graceless two-laned metal
with four-wheeled ferries
at a standstill waiting
for the light to change.
Fathers were stoic, gripping
leather, anticipating meatloaf
or chicken. Children were silent,
dull skies and flat clouds forward and aft.
Mothers hummed softly to a
crooner, voice made tinny
by rolled up windows and am radio.

Linda Laino

Poem at Sixty

Everything will break your heart

Blue wildflowers wilted in
the letter box, coffee
in bed smoking,
blue curls circling cracks
in the ceiling.

Everything will break

A blue note kept
faithful as a swallow
ochered and creased
with age whispers
wait for me.

Everything will

Two rose-colored petals
salvaged from the rubble
booked as a marker for
a life barely a flutter flash.

It all will break

Words fisted then offered now
spun to the wind,
a cadmium umbilicus
wound around lives lived and stilled
still, loved just the same.

It all will break.
Your heart.
Everything.

You must allow it.

Alan Walowitz

What's Worse

—October 27, 1962

Whatever I felt I feared
and that night it was in the air.
My father wanted bread for supper
and I was sent out in the thick of it,
not knowing to go fast or slow,
and which might make it worse— .
my folks and their demands,
the big kids who hung all night in the Woods
ready to shake me down,
the Russian missiles aimed
right at my heart—and any moment now.
What did I ever do?—and what's worse,
who'd be left to tell my tale
on this the night the world would end—
a boy sent on his own to Seligman's
to buy a seeded rye—make sure it's sliced thin?

I wouldn't starve.
I had the bread,
the caraway stuck in my teeth,
the sourness to remind me of home,
where I'd never arrive.
Might as well have the taste
in my mouth of what little I'd been
while rolling through the heavens,
one moment tangling with dad,
the next wrestling with God—or, what's worse,
maybe we'd all be blown to bits—
I hadn't even said a word—
and I'd never get to feel anything at all.

David B. Prather

Journal Entry: What Keeps Me Up at Night

There is no recipe, no cutouts or clippings
        my grandmother left in a kitchen drawer,
the occasional hand-written list of items

and directions, her script precise and clear.
        It's midnight, and I hunger for her vegetable
soup—carrots, potatoes, celery. Cabbage

brings it all together. Black pepper
        makes it warm. Tomato juice I put up
last year, the heirlooms of my garden,

leaves residue up the sides of the stewpot.
        a few pats of butter mellow as root, leaf,
legume, and kernel soften in the simmer.

I love the feel of a knife in my hand as I slice
        and chop, the tap of the blade against
the cutting board. There's no meat in the mix,

in honor of my vegetarian grandmother
        who grew up on a farm where animals were
slaughtered, the brutality that changed her.

Sometimes, when I can't sleep, I light
        the burners and cook my childhood
memories. I remember a dog barking,

a porch light, a bobcat at the edge of the yard
        where forest was a hodgepodge of shadow
and sycamore and moldering leaves.

I remember being told to stay inside.
        I think I sat at the kitchen window all night
to see if some other wild creature might

stalk me. I had a bowl of soup to lean over,
        steam rising around my face. Even now,
I look out my own window as all this

comes to a boil. Nothing moves near.
        Not even a moth to batter itself
upon glass panes. To try to become

one with the light I leave on throughout
        the night. I don't know why I do this.
Maybe the bobcat was just a symbol.

Maybe I'm remembering it all wrong.

Michael Minassian

My Friend, Eddie

My childhood friend Eddie
called the other day,
It's your turn, he said,
then hung up.

It took me a while
to figure out
what he meant.

When we were kids,
we dug a hole in the space
under his front porch
and buried his father's
chess set, some marbles
and a dead goldfish—

The week before,
his father had walked out,
vowing never to return.

Eddie stopped
feeding the goldfish,
and smashed the marbles
with a hammer.

When his mother saw us
under their front porch,
she asked what we were doing.

Digging a hole to China,
Eddie replied.

She nodded her head,
be careful, she barked,
then went back in the house
to have another drink.

A few years later, Eddie and I
had an argument over a girl,
and he punched me.

I just looked at him
and walked away;
we never spoke again.

I guess that's what
he was talking about
when he called
all those years later.

At some point,
time stands still,
circles around,
and catches us
at the back door.

Michael Estabrook

Philosophy

When I was younger
I'd walk the train tracks beyond
where we lived pondering
the direction of my life
where have I been?
where am I going?
what am I doing or not doing?
what could I be doing better?
Even though I'm older now
and still have no answers
to these my life's questions
I no longer tread the tracks
to ponder them
because those big trains appear silently
from around the bend awfully fast.

Daniel Edward Moore

At The Corner of Heavy and Acquaintance

Somewhere, someone
                is so tired of you,
the sound of your name
                makes them heavy with acquaintance.

Heavy as in a metal jock strap
                protecting them from longing.
Heavy as in when hearing hello
                their spine becomes a cobra.

Remind me, again, why my hand
                cut a hole in your throat:
object removal, a flower vase,
                a window your heart could
escape through at night
                to teach the world a lesson?

Tenderness rarely occurs to me
                at the hour you shame the moon,
turning it yellow as a caution light,
                where you decide you can't decide
if you have the power to shine.

I wish the end were different,
                beauty blooming instead of rocks
in a grave beneath your chin,
                words falling down the stem of your neck
in the window of a store on a street we loved
                where faces stopped to listen.

Rebecca Brock

Preop

The surgery room, after the bustle and baby talk
of the prep, is a bright unremarkable surprise.
Also cold. Masks and hats looming. The old look older,
I assume, because I know the small look smaller,
the vulnerable—well, I am only allowed back
because I am the mother and the medical staff
are doing camaraderie, the wink and the nudge
and the friendly, friendly fire before the undoing,
before repairing the undone. It is hard for me
to act as though it is not hard to be alive—
my boy is stiff and terrified and breathing quick,
willing himself to hold, to stay still.
Even still, he grimaces at the anesthesia mask,
and I reach to help hold it—
Well aren't you useful, mom, someone says.
I mumble something back but that's the whole of me—there—
holding the mask and he's trying not to go under,
his eyes trying to open up against their closing,
he pants *into* the mask—fighting—
and I'm telling him—this child, this boy
whom I've taught everything from look both ways,
to pedal, pedal, pedal, to c-a-t cat, to 1 plus 1,
to wash your hands, brush your teeth, wash
your parts, don't hug your friends so hard,
say please, say thank you, look people in the eye
when you speak—*breathe, buddy, just breathe*—
he fights until it seizes him,
the easy drift a hard crash.
I say what all the mothers must say: *he's really special*
and find myself making thank you hands, pleading prayer
hands, please and thank you and God bless hands—

two of the nurses can't meet my eyes, one is crying,
maybe other mothers
are tougher, maybe nurses
understand, more than most,
or maybe it was just him,
that last fight he gave before going out,
that spirit: its pulse and serve,
its oddity and fight.

Sandy Coomer

Letter to Beth from Vermont

It's snowing again.
I asked a man in the laundromat
if it ever stops snowing in Vermont.
He said not this week, and we watch
our flannel shirts and wool socks spin.
Snow makes me lonely, all the white
space of it, the blank page I want
to crush with my fur-lined boots.
I'm not made for cold, like you say
you are, now that night bends across
your face like a black wing. You used
to sing. Your words used to spark
the wild tangle in both of us until
your tongue was clipped and you
trembled in the dark. I told you
to live for love and love betrayed you,
swallowed the sweet curve of your hand
like an owl gulps mice. I told you
to live for joy and joy let you chase it
for a while, then folded its arms
and fell asleep. What can I tell you then
about this snow that you'll believe
except that when I step outside and sink
to my knees, it's a kind of prayer
that holds me up. When I blink
the whiteness back to color, I see
what's clean and possible, a field un-
broken, the curved crest of frosted hills.
Don't worry if this note arrives damp
or the ink smeared. I added a handful
of snow to the envelope so you can see
what I see—all the beautiful crystals
laid out flat in your palm.

Jeff Burt

Playing Trumpet After the Lights Go Off

When I kiss the feet of my baby
and blow on the bottom of his feet,
you may mistake the tapping of my fingers
on his ankles for rim-drumming,
not hear the valves of the trumpet
with lips pursed, embouchure firm,
a fanfare before I powder
and swaddle and place a kiss
on each of his misdirected eyes,
lashes like the shadows of trees
filtering the suddenness of light,
my muted close, a soft glissando
before the worn velvet stop.

John Grey

The Women

My father slapped me on the back.
muttered something about "women",
and then placed a fishing pole
gently into my hands
as if he was putting
a wedding ring on my finger.

Down by the lake, late afternoon,
we were the real couple,
backs firm against tree trunk,
lines taut, silent but for
those times when he mumbled some
more about not being able to
figure out "your mother" followed
by more silence and then
an "or your sisters."

With him as teacher,
I so easily accepted
that fish would bite,
that women were the font
of all I couldn't comprehend,
all I would never know.

At sundown,
we'd gather up our catch
and go home.
If we were lucky,
it'd be fish dinner that night.
The women would prepare it.
I still don't know how.

Michael Estabrook

Still Listening

So Dad didn't die when he was only 36
Dr. Zullo gave him an experimental drug
that rolled the stomach cancer back out to sea

And Mom didn't marry that jackass pencil salesman
with his shotguns and beehives
and his big stupid Lincoln Town Car

She and Dad came around a lot and spoiled
the grandchildren taking them to the movies and ball games
and out fishing like our grandparents spoiled us

And Dad was there when we needed him for advice
and to diagnose the problems with our cars
simply by cocking his head and listening

Jeff Burt

Bean Creek

Summer leaves hang like rags and a hot wind dehydrates.
Hydrangeas slump like old men after a long lunch. By morning
    they will rise.

I've stepped into the dwindling creek and luck tickles my feet,
a crawdad clawing for a moor finds my big toe, clamps, holds.

My children dabble with sticks downstream making alphabets
in the sand that disappear as they are written except the Capital L.

Ferns rise out of dirt like small pineapples.
Flexing strength, firs raise their own roots.

Hangers on, my father writes, of death even the faithful fear,
hold resolute to life, hoping they will be bypassed.

And here as well, suspended from the sepia shine of the sunset,
all life sticks to another, fronds and their hidden spores attached to
    white socks

hoping to bloom next spring in the fragments of dark soil,
the crawdad now pocketed between worn boulders,

my wife leading me by hand from the creek up the steep trail
into the last light pouring from the foundry ladle of the sky.

Carol Lynn Stevenson Grellas

Turning the Car Around

When I'm driving my car,
I still hear my dad's voice
say, *turn around sweetie, follow*
that guy on the motorcycle.
he knows the way, as if there was
some kind of grand payoff for
following a stranger in any direction
other than the one we were already
going. But that was his dementia
taking over and I knew better
than to listen to an old man whose head
was overrun with madness
and by the time I could have
explained it to him, he'd long forgotten
he'd ever questioned which route to take
home or that there was another way
to anywhere even here.
But now that he's gone I wish at least
once I'd done what he'd asked,
followed that guy on the motorcycle
as if that guy knew the way, that guy
with the wind at his back and his engine
revved up with the rebellious sun gleaming
down like a flare in the middle the road
and our fumbling so desperately as we tried
to navigate those last few months of his life
and the loss of his memories,
and all that we hoped to hang onto
like some kind of desperate salvation
or escape from reality where the familiar
might keep us safe since neither of us
knew where the hell we were going.

Cynthia Anderson

The Far Pavilions

Dad's owned the hardback
for decades, and now he's cracked
it again, reading the entire tome
for the fourth time—finding
comfort in the slow pace,
the familiar story and characters,
the foreignness of India—a way
to forget the catheter, the full bag
of urine slumped on the floor,
the slow decline on hospice.
He's engulfed by the recliner,
a distant look in his eyes.
It helps to repeat what's come
before, and to hear clatter
from the kitchen next door,
happy voices that carry
no hurtful memories.
Blink, and he's a toddler
in a sailor suit, solitary,
aching for friends
he never had.

Gary Beaumier

Wordplay with Rock

There was the summer
I harvested rocks
from the beach.
Sand pumiced my feet
and the water painfully cold.

There was the day
my boy came home
after all those years
only to take a hit
and unravel everything
and all I could do was watch.

…and at season's end
I drank coffee
under unleafing trees
weighted yet spectral
with stars piercing down.

I wondered how it works
with rock.
Does it crackle
when you flame the butane
into the bowl?
Does the euphoria
slam into you
exactly eight seconds
after you suck it into your lungs?

After eight years
did you get back
that righteous high

or are you chasing it still?
And will you keep chasing it
until you are under a rock?

Did you think
I didn't goddamn care?

Sandy Coomer

Child on a Balcony in Assisi

Back streets always have eyes
and yours hold the morning open.

A tightrope of space
on your tiny balcony, you grip

the bars with fingers straight
from your mouth, the lick

and taste of your world.
Will you remember me,

my American wave, and how
my pause gave you permission

to tuck your chubby face
behind your arms? You stayed

like the morning, a little longer
curdled into thought and became

an image I hold, its blushed moment
a fragment of focused faith.

Maybe you already see
this world is a balance of shadows

and what we claim as real
is only our version of truth.

Looking down, did you see the same
morning that I saw looking up,

and in that frame and capture, did I see
the same you as you will one day be?

Your dark umber eyes blink the future
awake. Wonder unfurls and washes

the soul-stung cobblestones
hobbled with grief.

What would this balcony be
without you but a sliver of rock

gripping an empty sleeve of space?
And what would I be but a man

still restless, still looking up,
eyes searching, hands empty.

This is the pedal steel's
low wail of sweet longing,
the open tuning. . .

—Gary Glauber, "Errand Boy"

Seth Jani

Repast

You crafted love
Part from desire
And part from the body's
Movable forms.
After the leavening force of grief
You couldn't believe
It had always been a simple light
Moving through the rooms
With the grace of summer.
Maybe the difficulties
We encounter in each other's eyes
Are just misunderstandings.
Facing strangers, it's hard to believe
We are all the universe
Spinning beautifully
Across the distance.
But here we are,
Wind and flame,
Sharing this delicate bread.

Sandy Coomer

Anniversary

The year finished the first slow circle
of missing you, and just as you predicted

the daffodils returned with a harvest of gold.
The hillside is ripe for gathering.

You waited until spring to die, until the earth
expanded to accept your body in a cradle of green.

Come back.

You've been too long gone and the ache you said
would ease, hasn't. The pangs you said would cease

wrecking the bright new joys of *without-you* days
still sharpen their teeth in the stillness of night.

What's not to like about returning?

The snow is gone and the koi are awake
flashing orange and white in the pond.

The path to the meadow that harbored
the small herd of deer needs clearing.

Trillium and bloodroot wait for your cry of discovery.
Peonies long for your bouquet.

I know you think I'm fine, that I haven't counted
each day as one more to endure.

Would you be surprised to find I've forgotten
how to laugh, that winter left me unbearably cold?

I've done what you asked. I donated your books,
your clothes. I haven't missed a day walking the dog.

Come help me plant lettuces and tie the blackberries
to their stakes, and pick out new roses to plant by the fence.

The daffodils spread tender yellow against the grass.
You and I once walked together there.

Come back now. It's only fair.

Kersten Christianson

You Choose Your Solitude

It's easy to live with nothing.

The kitchen without a table
the phone number
nobody calls.

Is it so easy?

In Klukshu the snow
curls and gathers,
blankets a far-flung
highway.

Is it so easy?

Yes. Cleave
your world in two,
the halves of a grapefruit
made whole. Your scrawled
name in the snow.

Steve Klepetar

The Language of Stars

If only I could have spoken your name
in the language of stars,
your music might have flowed from the hills
like a river being born.
That would have been a miracle,
a way of opening the sky.
If only I could have whispered
your name in the language of goats or crows.
What a world would have emerged,
a tiny egg growing, then floating on the sea.
If only I could have turned in my chair,
with my eyes nailed to your voice
and your hair, with my hands on fire,
with my parched tongue drinking in the rain.

Tamara Madison

To a Grieving Friend

When Grief with its dark bulk
bars your friend's door,
there are no right words.

In time, Grief will lie down,
close one eye and then the other.

That is when you will hear
my heart, dear friend, drumming
low and steady just outside.

Carl Boon

Thrall

We supposed the pin-oaks
on our acre's edge
would age with us, and so carried
their adjectives close by—
slender and graceful,
then stately, then sad.
It's been twelve years
since the cancer in your breast
appeared and receded—
a moth at sunset—
twelve years since we drank
champagne on the porch
and told each other God
was merciful and listening.
Now the news arrives again—
a mass, four millimeters only,
but near the bone, and you
must cough and go in blankets
room to room without me.
I make soup in the afternoon,
and you witness pines
instead of pin-oaks.
I don't know why. The meds,
the slants of light, August
unbecoming to us all.
The worst of cancer isn't death,
but that it carries us
to undreamed places: this
stairway, this fireplace
where yesterday in anger
you burned seven photographs
of the land we once called ours.

Peter Leight

Personally I'm Balancing a Lot of Things,

shifting my weight in the lateral or sagittal direction to keep from drifting to the side. I'm feeling a little shaky, which is often what balance is like. Sometimes I close my eyes and breathe deeply, first one way then the other like a kind of stereo, letting my head drop down and lifting it up. Leaning both ways like a canoeist—when you turn to the side the other side starts turning, I'm not sure what the technical term is. I mean there are attractions on both sides, not one or the other, like a herringbone. We often move one way in order to avoid moving another, holding our hands together and pulling them apart, as if alternating between attachment and inattention. There are also times when there's too much on one side and not enough on the other—we usually end up with less of what we need more of. When we're together you're on one side while I'm on the other, you don't have to warn me beforehand. People need to be together when they're apart, and when they're together they start moving away from each other—there isn't a statement with a balance at the end you don't bother to check anymore because it's always been right before.

William Doreski

The End of Evolution

Hiking in a rave of blackflies,
I'm slight enough to pass unseen
among the ghosts of animals
extinguished by the ice age.
You wonder that I wonder
at the boulders the glaciers left,
the trees half-gnawed by beavers,
the dead pine splintered by the ant-
crazed hammering of a redhead
pileated woodpecker. Why scratch
dimpled bug bites when paintings
by Matisse flourish in the mental
gallery, and music by Sibelius
flutters in the cusp of my hearing?
Shouldn't I slump in an armchair
and let these hauntings consume me
the way aesthetes of the previous
century self-consumed by smoking
bitter cigarettes and drinking
green liqueurs from fragile cups?
You'd rather see me flourish
a flimsy yellowed paperback
than pose on the rocks at the edge
of a pond the color of clouds.
So we differ in style and gender,
just as the boulders vary
in mineral content, and the pond
shifts mood and stance with the light.
When the mammoth went extinct
some distant prenatal notion
of myself also went extinct,
and now I'd like to recover it
by tracking myself backward years

and years, long before I met you,
long before we mistook ourselves
for the end of evolution,
two gestures sculpted with joy.

Marc Swan

Whiplash

If this were the hold of a sailing
ship on a rocky sea of wind
and change, I'd understand pitch-
black darkness of the room,
tom-tom beat of my heart. A monitor
lights my way as I type these simple
words. She's asleep upstairs.
After the accident a month ago,
she rests most of the day, gets up,
feels good, pushes herself to do more,
falls back into bed, exhausted
by once minimal effort. She's here
when I go to work, when I come home
for lunch, when I return from work
she is on the patio, on the couch,
or in bed resting. The neurologist
said the injury was like a sprained
ankle in her head. I try to imagine
muscle tissue supporting my brain
wrenched to one side—whipped
this way and that. I want to take her
away from this new routine, a pattern
knitted out of boredom, fed on disuse,
fly on a big jet to a small place
with a cottage for two, river nearby,
salmon leaping out of running water.
We could walk in the woods, find
a grassy knoll for a picnic, touch
like we haven't touched in a long time.

George Franklin

Clean Sheets

I just made the bed with clean sheets. They're
Wrinkled but washed and fresh smelling, the
Weave a little rough against my hands.
When you get here, I'll fix coffee, yours
With steamed milk, foamy, mine dark,
Tasting of burnt sugar, reminding
Me of the night sky in another
Latitude, that neighborhood where we
Walked, the moon still not up over the
Hills, the low rooftops, hotel signs, and
Shuttered windows, from somewhere voices,
Music, a dog barking behind a
High white wall, my lips touching your neck.
After dinner, we'll turn back the sheets,
Slip in beside each other, our days
Still with us, scents we can't get rid of,
Sandalwood clinging to your nightgown,
Lemon peel, onions on my fingers.
When we touch, we could be anywhere.

Carl Boon

Walpurgis

Not all the gods are dead.
Some bring us beers in squat glasses,
still shining. I hold

Ilse's hand and carry her past
one hundred goblins and seven old
wizards. The trees scream for us

to stop and the marigolds—burnt
butter—lean at us. The holy ends here,
a forest edge in a Faustus scene.

I tell Ilse the gods love us
for a day, at least, and her hair rises,
a cornucopia of sin and stuff

from books forgotten.
We are going to make a baby now
and call her Dreaddark Patter

or Wholesome Rot, for it's Friday
after Sunday and Jesus is a star now,
a man for a Christmas card or Whitsun

frown. I feel myself being born
and rising and it doesn't matter
if night's an avalanche. We are happy

as shadows, lingering, wailing,
looking out upon the music
that carries us home.

Gary Beaumier

Night Forest

Once there was a woman in the night forest
who could hear above the register of most.
She would listen to mice sing in chorus
or coyotes comfort their young
over the flash and rumble of coming weather.

There was the night when I stayed in the garden
late into the hours and you called for me
and together we watched the gods
toss stars across the sky and later
we returned to our bed and I watched you
over the vastness of our pillows
as your breathing fell into a rhythm
and you separated from me.

Have your dreams returned you to a wooded place,
dusted in moonlight, where you keen your ears
to other selves, selves beyond the register of my knowing?

Jessica Mehta

The Weight of Secrets

Secrets weigh a tremendous lot
so you have to be real sure
you can bear the brunt.
And that they're worth it—like a child
who cries something so fierce
you rock them to quiet, something
like complacency. Heavy burdens
only strengthen tendons, grow
muscles, densify bones so long
before the joints give out. I've carried
so many pinky swears they've built colonies
on my back. A dowagers hump
of things I'll never tell, words packed
with a blistering power my tongue
would burn before those syllables
can trickle fire down my chin.

Daniel Edward Moore

The Affair

During the affair I had with myself,
black roses, red wine, one dish in the sink,

always exhausted by long drives to nowhere,
by hours spent starting and stopping my heart.

It was solitude's privilege to wrap me in frost,
to find me naked and scared in the yard,

pretending the moon was the face of god,
pitted with worry. the size of my fears.

Raising the flag on the cold steel box,
just so someone would stop, anger

with a beard would yell from his truck.
I knew I was being unfaithful, knew

I would feed the fire with stamps
to save me from adultery's sticky return.

Phill Provance

Hours

To St. Pious,
defender from too many cigarettes,
let me not smoke the lucky too soon,
nor let me set
off the fire alarm
in any airport restrooms,
nor let the butts
in my overfull ashtrays
fall to the floor smoldering
beside my particleboard bookshelf.
(Please note: especially remember
this final favor when
I am reading on the toilet.)

✝
To St. Raphael,
succor for the good sex,
let not my left nut
know what my right is doing.
Preserve me from the stranger
but also from brown mystery growths.
And lead me not into titty bars
with girls whose hand jobs
give patrons a Brazilian
contact STD that makes a guy's
dick shed like a garter snake.

✝
To St. Thomas More,
fiery sword of divorce attorneys,
sow nothing less than chain lightning
in my lawyer's eyes. Transform her

into Kali, Boudicca and Xena,
Joan of Arc and Pallas Athena,
all infused into one tangerine pantsuit.
Let her tongue spit venomous
dropkicks before the bench.
Let her words erupt
with an atomic Kung-Fu grip.
Let her protect me
like my own mother.

✝

To St. Rita,
sister to the lonesome,
let not my despondency over her
who once shot through my breath,
once made me believe
I would drown as our hands grazed,
consume me in the rituals of heartbreak;
remember me to mornings
and the sweetness of sunlight
through the curtains of my tiny studio,
even when she is no longer
warmed beside me.

✝

To St. Felicitous,
patron of the small and lost,
let me still be the vanquisher
of burnt-out nightlights
and slayer of gray reflections
he spies in closets,
under beds and down dark hallways
until, someday, I am that grizzled face
whose hand he squeezes
as he huddles over the paper-white
sheets where my breath
shudders and breaks.

Betsy Mars

The Return of the Termites

After it was agreed
that things had gone too far,
we brought in outside counsel.

By now every surface was covered
in grit, termites defecating
bits of what was left of our home.

They came with drills and chemicals
in masks and goggles, teetered
on ladders, did whatever they did
to repair the holes.

We rested assured the blight was gone.

Two months later we find them
on an August day beating wings
on the cool tile floor, in the hamper,
in the drawers.

One catches in my clothes.
More swim the shallows of the shower,
fallen from the overheated rafters.

I wield the spray
and wash them down the drain.
The next day there are more.

The structure is being eaten,
the beams are weakened.

Suddenly we find ourselves falling
through the foundation,
our marriage collapsing
while we were busy looking elsewhere.

Gary Glauber

Errand Boy

I carry out the trash
and with it an unburdening
of suburban responsibilities,
careful care of tended lawn,
the weight of native souls long gone
from formerly forested high ground.

I am haunted with
afflictions of love. desires
to simplify mortgage
and insurance shackles,
shady cloud formations
slow dancing across
fading cerulean sky.

This is the pedal steel's
low wail of sweet longing,
the open tuning that invites
unassuming ear to listen.
This is how weeds invade
gardens, how those sporting antlers
make scant winter meals last,
how lush growth morphs into
bright blinding bleak terrain.

I sing along with coyote pack's yowls,
gooseflesh raised in reflexive salute,
bloodlust of the wild unleashed
toward unsuspecting moon.
Martyrs of the makeshift unite,
sliding over black ice toward
dark inevitable, eyes closed
to hymn of engine thrum,
careening anthem-like chorus
calling Aeolus from afar.

Rust never oxidizes here
and everything stays just so,
Currier and Ives with an
insider's nod and wink.
The cans at end of driveway
innocuous bystanders like
ancient seers, lifted and emptied,
but back again brimful with insight
same time the very next week.

Peter Leight

History of Future Blowup

When we blew out the candles we didn't see anything, nothing at all, we don't even know how to make exceptions—it's a form of fair-mindedness we often admire in others. I actually think we're more accessible to others than we are to ourselves, do you think it's true? At the same time we were under pressure we were pressing at about the same time, when you emptied the fridge and didn't even bother to fill it up I didn't stop eating, I'm not interested in retaliation, seriously what's the point? Not arguing—it's embarrassing to argue, it's not worth it, we're not even hungry at the same time. Pressing in on one side and pushing out on the other, I actually think we're agreeing with each other. At the same time we started taking up more space, I'm not even sure how it happened—of course the future is different from the past in the same way as the past is different from the past, do you see what I mean? First you start pressing, then you're under pressure, pressing on each other like a fitting, squeezing out the little spitballs of juice. Then the wind settled in between us and blew out all the candles, pressing out from a point between us and pushing us out at the same time, blowing us away from each other like a kind of self-defense—when you're not hungry I'm not going to stop eating.

Steve Klepetar

Now You Are One

> *fly in the wind of the dead*
> *above me, float on the water*
> *of my dreams.* —Yehuda Amichai,

So many dead, and now you are one,
gone into that pale throng so quietly
I almost missed your slipping,
the last breath hovering above your bed.
I come to the street of restaurants,
all those smells lingering,
cilantro and garlic and roasting meat.
You ate so little, and always the same foods –
yogurt and a little cheese,
chicken drowned in a pot with paprika
that lasted many meals,
and always cookies, two at a time all day.
You gave away as many as you ate,
sweet little bribes you banked for favors.
Now all you eat is wind.
May that fill you, so you remain with the stars,
with the hawks wheeling across the sky,
with the stream floating by my house
as I dream you back into your body,
your rusty voice repeating the same prayers,
the same dreams you said were never coming true.

Stan Sanval Rubin

Two-and-a-Half Years

If I had half the magic
I thought I was born with,
I would never have let you die.

I would have screamed hatred
at the cells we both hated
until nothing was left of them

and everything could go back
to the way it was before
the sky filled with your absence.

If I had the courage
to say what I grieve for,
I would say I understand grief

the way a prisoner
understands good bread,
the kind he will never taste

until taste itself doesn't matter.
I would know where
the light goes and the dark goes

inside our bodies.
I would know why
grief brings no wisdom

but we have it anyway.
I would know who is writing this.
At least, that.

Donna Hilbert

Dear Sadness,

You live in a saddlebag
cinched to my hip
by sinew and bone.
To walk with you is hard.
Please, forgive my complaint.
Others hurt more, I know.
When you were fixed
between atlas and axis
like a petrified necklace,
I hurt more.
It was hard to hold up,
impossible to turn.

Sean Kelbley

Cancer's Back

This time, a jacked-up pickup truck
off-roading through your innermost
interior. At the chemo suite

I hold your hand and watch you fill
with necessary poison. This is the last
defense. Already you've been excavated

like the Love Canal. Irradiated.
Inside my wallet is a picture from before,
you as a panoply of muscled vistas—

preserved, maintained with weights and
cardio and filtered water, antioxidants
and yoga and the right amount of

sleep—you as good steward
to a landscape. Our trip out West,
remember? Assholes ruined that, too:

a frat kid, back turned to the silent lip
of the Grand Canyon, screaming *Gimme
french fries* into withered Arizona; scabby

arms in Colorado, tossing garbage from a
Jeep Grand Cherokee to both sides of the
Continental Divide. Noisy trash. It just

shows up, and thumps and woofs and
tweets its tribal code to all the other freaks
through speakers piled high behind

the cab. It yells *Let's party!* It goes coal-rolling. It wants to turn each desert into Burning Man.

Duncan Richardson

The Wind
after Sylvia Plath's "Winter Trees"

The wind is the storm's tongue.
We feel its kiss
its probing passion
its slippery desire for us.

It taunts us
with the flamenco
of the plastic bag.

Trees thrill to it
grasses swoon and sway
clouds run headless
                       heedless
birds hide their wings
from the lick of it.

I watch how it takes your hair
in a curling tip
tasting your colours
               silver, jet and bronze

and I wave it on
holding out my hands
for a touch of bliss

Lachlan Brooks

Quick Glance at Eurydice

Stains, again, on things that easily stain,
the uniform kinds of stains, all one, all same
but for the histories of each, the blame,
the blamelessness of ancient times,
of yesterdays just past where every pain
is simple fact and simple blame, where
time is only galleries of fame, and glances
over shoulders, outlawed, have siren-calls
towards a simple fall, a spell that's cast
on all that came before; nothing truly lasts
at all, and time makes ribbons of the past.

Carl Boon

Widow

She'll have made coffee, shaken
the crumbs from the placemats.

The light from the south window's
enough to read by—

no matter the radio, the children
chattering stories that were mine.

I cannot know my mother's loneliness,
how she feels making coffee

among the sounds of sparrows—
she's not home.

Nor would she wish to be,
because the house is just a house

where she used to be a wife, joyful,
problematic, handsome. Rich

with the hours of night stitched
before her. The kids have gone

with troubles to live into, meanderings
of love and what is not,

what matters and what can't, here
and there among the living breathing.

The piano is a shelf for pictures,
the rooms too many to clean.

Tamara Madison

The Great Sea

A Buddhist once said each life
is a river branching off a larger river,
and every river flows in its own path
to the great sea that is death.
I imagine my parents in that sea –
his bear-arms pulling side stroke,
pale legs scissoring the green tide,
her in a flowered swim cap doing
an Esther Williams churn –
one stroke face down, one stroke up.
I doubt they've even looked
for one another there; now, each one
visits me. Even on this chilly morning
I feel the circles of their separate
embraces, hers close – I can almost
feel her spirit-breath – his wide
as a ring of Saturn. Now
they've swum off far
into that great sea; may it keep them
ever cycling on its currents back to me.

Joe Cottonwood

All of your ancestors come to your wedding

By horse, by canoe they come
dressed in grass skirts and beaver pelt hats.
They bring amphorae of wine,
barrels of ancient beer.

They fight. Belch. Kiss both cheeks.
They paint designs on your face
and weave flowers in your hair.
They hug, squeeze, make ribald jokes.

They smoke sacred herbs. Chant,
pound on drums, sing in lost language.
They puff music in hollowed bamboo,
dance in circles, juggle flaming torches.
They draw antelope on the walls of your cave.

As dowry they bring generations of struggle,
millenniums of sacrifice. They will come
to your wedding whether you invite them or not.

Wish them welcome.

Judy Kronenfeld

Explosion

Decades together, yet still
white phosphorus in our chests.
Who strikes first? Does it matter?
We are each tinder.

A word misread as a missile
on either's radar—
and bombers rip
placid skies.

Afterwards, scorched, exhausted,
we both dig in and stoke the embers
in private underground shelters
flanking the de facto DMZ.

But we grow chilled and forlorn,
and crawl out of
our cellars, and creep back
across the landscape
we've laid waste

to lie, wordless, in each other's
arms—as if just awakening
from the same shocking nightmare,
in the only place of safety
and warmth.

Stuart Stromin

A Supper for Banquo

The old oyster-beds,
of sunken wire and splinters
along the coast of Normandy,
stretched out for flat miles
of mud,
to the vague silver horizon.

But I never could imagine
where the high tide went;
or why
you could prefer
another man's love,
in the evenings
when I was still so handsome.

In my mouth,
like a block of dirty ice,
I surrendered
to the taste of lobsters and Muscadet
in the beach-front brasseries,
where the sea-breeze
with a whiff of silt
swept off the promenade,
and we were speaking
French which the Parisians
could not understand.

I would not know
what things to do
now,
on another night with you,
not even how to stay warm
in the spaces,

where the steely wind
invades between the palm trees.

I never recognized the figures on the roadside,
patient as statues,
I never saw the blades.

Even the hungry travelers
keep far from the banquet,
aloof as backwash.

Dan Sicoli

forced smile

perhaps she'll wake
before noon
before the sun is crowned

and yet something in me
grows
boisterous

"let her lay" you say
but it's trying
for me

i want her to
own the dawn
like a barnyard rooster
or that damn Jack Russell across the street

it's true
she's earned
the quiet
and reprieve

and so
i tread
soft-shoed

Stuart Stromin

Hourglass

Schoolchildren lie
with their backs to the grass,
chests open to the tilted heaven,
discovering shapes in the puffy clouds.

Warm foam like a lace veil rushes to the beach.
The enthusiasm of fate propels the brimming tide.

On the crisscross of checkered tablecloths,
there are faint stains of the damp, half-finished rings
that beer-mugs print,
after nights of endless conversation.

We knew we had a lifetime to cheat death.

But it looks like snow,
stealing the greenery from the peaks.
It looks like snow, tugging down
the bright sky.
It is falling, falling frozen
on our youth and on our age
as cold and as white
and as dangerously beautiful
as a bride in her glorious gown.

And now my old friend keeps vigil
at his father's death-bed,
counting down the minutes,
like flakes of frost,
like grains of sand.

Marc Swan

End of the Season

Leaves have fallen, no snow yet
but predicted later today. Wind picks
up as I walk down the rutted road
to the bay. In the small dirt lot
a white Volvo station wagon, an older
couple wrapped up in conversation.
They don't look my way as I pass by.
On the rear bumper and window —
create the world you want to live in,
Give Peace a Chance. Ahead of me
a shell fishermen knee deep in muck,
waders caked with brown ooze, pulling
a small water sled with a basket of clams.
I remember those days in high rubber boots
out of the kayak in Barnstable Harbor,
low tide, small islands jutting up, raking
through slick humps for little necks,
steamers. I start my half mile trek home
passing the Volvo. They are quiet now —
like the decision has been made. I think
of a piece in the Press Herald, a couple
up the coast, seventy-five, seventy-seven,
on their bed, hands held, watching waves
ebb and flow, waiting for the bourbon
and barbiturates to kick in.

John Leonard

As Seen on T.V.

Robotic fish, wearing a plastic halo and angel wings;
mounted on a wooden plaque and probably Made in China.
Something for a dad to hang on his office wall. A button
on the side that, if you press it, the fish starts singing
"Earth Angel" by Marvin Berry & The Starlighters.
But the button only gets pressed maybe once or twice—
Once on Christmas morning when the dad unwraps it
and seems so amused and grateful because it's Christmas
and also because he is on his third cranberry mimosa.
And a second time, years later, when he pulls his wife
into his office on the very first evening that none of the kids
are home; everyone off to college, living their own lives.
He presses the button almost as a joke, and the Duracells
awaken the fish who suddenly fills the room with music.
So they dance for 30 seconds, pressed together, as the air becomes
heavy with novelty, laughter, and slow tears; mouthing the words
to a song heard one other time, when heaven seemed further away.

When the music falls
from the twin-blooming trees
it's like water stirring in a place
that's been so still for years.

—Seth Jani, "Birdwatching"

Cynthia Anderson

The Interior

No one lives there—too remote,
merciless, a place for outlaws

in hiding, not meant to sustain
human life. The wind can rend

skin from flesh, the cold take
your eyes. Yet you yearn for

this waste of glacier and desert,
volcano and lake—an untamed

wilderness shaped like a heart.
Something waits for you

on the knife-edge of danger—
the chance to be someone

else. The chance you might
not return. The chance

earth herself might sing
in a voice you can hear.

David B. Prather

Expulsion

Gardens hush with evening,
foliage strapped with darkness
and the sort of quiet that speaks
with other voices—strong, clear,
passionate voices—the only song of night
we will ever know. We are surprised
that something has waited all day
to compose this nocturne.
Caddisflies, springtails, assassin bugs.
We don't even know the bodies
out there, like ghosts
pulled up from wet grasses.
We cannot decipher the messages
clattering one over the other to reach us
as we sleep. Blister beetles,
checkerspots, and mourning cloaks.
They carve their disenchantment
even over a world of our own creation—
the brazen drone of street lights,
the hum of car engines three streets over,
the bombast of town after town
filling every valley, every copse,
every riverbed and flood plain, moving
through each tributary, ridge and rock.
Ichneumons, earwigs, hawkmoths.
We hear the brief joining of short lives.
We hear anxiety rubbing out of every wing,
every leg, and every mandible.
Each life is so common to its place, its time,
its inherent and unpreventable behavior.
Carrion beetles, army worms, and walking sticks.
By morning, a shred of moon
clings like lint to the hem of the sky.

Again, we are sure that someone lay in our beds
beside us while we preoccupied ourselves
with one breath and another,
someone who would take us as we are,
never asking whether or not we were ready to go.

Vivian Faith Prescott

Acclimatization

She ground drifts with the wind overhead,
the first American generation Sámi Girl

A new study released

who's unable to command the wind.
She senses it there, though—

argues there is evidence that

all delicate things turn from her.
Between buildings, a deer in the alleyway

local winds are a more important factor,

lifts its head from its grazing.
occasionally she reaches up to embrace

claiming changes in wind direction and velocity

the curl of her fear,
in the rising particles of air.

unrelated to climate change.

She is filled with lightning
and thunderheads,

Note that the wind changes consistently,

and feels ready to burst at any moment,
but into what she doesn't know.

natural variability cannot be ruled out.

She occasionally swallows a thread of wind
and it spins her around

The wind acts to change

until she doesn't know which way to go next.
Her outer garment is her too thick illusions,

like sweat drying on the skin,

her insides tumble disharmonic.
She names these feelings,

a pretty simple story,

these moments that shift something inside her
toward the wild.

that's going to take people by surprise,

Call her a gradual adjustment of the body
to new climatic conditions,

pushing it in a warming direction.

or what her ancestors named campfire sparks
in wind—spirits-blown-about.

*Italics: Found lines from article "Study: Natural changes in wind
cause Pacific warming" by Jeff Barnard, Komo News.

Matthew James Friday

The Dipper

I caught you
scuttling off your rock
in the creek that slips
behind Morgins.

                      The frothy-white
wave of your breast
      gave you away.

For a moment you perched,

bobbing your territory

and then returned to silence

broken by a man
crossing the creek
and spitting into the water.

Stephen Black

Mostly Water

55 to 60%
to be almost exact

body planet

First floating inside our mothers

No matter what else we are
we are mostly water
endlessly murmurating

cloud rain stream river ocean vapor cloud

On a bank beside the river
the best thoughts are river thoughts

Like this:
shrews locusts eagles earthworms lions
oaks
even rocks swallow rain

And this:
We seek
something hard
to engrave ourselves upon
but

houses forests stones
dissolve

eventually.

Nothing remains
after us

but the water
we once held

that once held us

Like the bird sufficient
with its one unfurling song
the river sings only this.

Seth Jani

Birdwatching

From the body of the stone
I am searching for that yellow wing
Which haunts the sky,
The glimmer and incandescence
Which sparks on the dark pool
Of the pupil, as if a galaxy were
Exploding from inside.
We have many names
For the mysterious flash
Which rattles our lives
From their dull cages,
But no facts,
No designations beyond
The deep codes of fable.
When the music falls
From the twin-blooming trees
It's like water stirring in a place
That's been so still for years
Even the dead listen,
Raising their flayed heads
From the cold echo chambers
In the mire's dusky caves.

Vivian Faith Prescott

Indicators

There is mention of ambient noise,
how seals hide from killer whales

among the pop and burst of a melting glacier.
There are arguments concerning how high

we live above the present sea, how our tidal days
are spent with irregular fluctuations.

Old folks comment how the winter sky
has faded into a dull blue smoke.

But all this talk weighs less than a season
of dust and who am I to question

this weeping we have awakened.
Every week I participate in a familiar rite—

rebuilding my seawall, washing sea spray
from my living room windows,

knowing there is a time-honored way
we revel the sea lingering in our lungs

and its rinsing of our wounds.

Judy Kronenfeld

Coming Up from Under, after Surgery for Multiple Breaks

At first you're pushing up against heavy, dark
water, for what feels like far too many seconds,
though a few hours before you were dropped
into it, abruptly, as if it were luxurious
and soft as feathers into which to fall
and fall and fall without harm.
When you finally reach the light,
your eyes fluttering and re-closing,
your body's weightless as a floater's
in the sea, shallow ripples of cool drowsiness
washing over it. In these moments,
no replay of gravity's knife-at-the-back
yank, of the shatter of bones
like ice in a bag crushed
by a mallet. Freed
of your broken self, you ride
your own calm swells
of breathing, as if, at a distance,
you are watching healing weave—
from the crumbled inside out,
from the ravaged edges in.

Kersten Christianson

To the Bare Salmonberry Branch in Winter Cold
—After James Wright's "To the Saguaro Cactus Tree in the Desert Rain"

I'm not certain how tiny juncos
twitter and flit through your maze
of stalks.

I have tried to extricate myself from sharp-thorned
memory, that seems

tangled and impossible at night.
I wish to be the dark shadow
of raven, I wish I were
the slink of river otter
and the perched patience of eagle.
I have no idea how you summon
your spring greens,
blush of June bloom.
I shiver in winter near the sea,
the often rain,
so I quit.

Teach me to hope again.

Tamara Madison

Orchid Cactus

I rise to a sky of milky stillness,
yet the plants are moving quietly

in their roots in a gentle unfurling
of leaf, a lengthening of stem.

For everything all around and in us
moves this way. Teeth emerge

from gums, nails like tiny glaciers
crawl across the nail bed, and life

pushes us along its moody current
toward an endpoint which is just

another new unfurling in a tale
of atoms moving within molecules.

Observe the squirrel who stands
and twitches her tail beneath the arm

of the cactus that just now
is preparing its wands to open

the silken flames of its flowers
to the milk-white sky.

K.B. Ballentine

The Spirit of Wild

To sing in the dark
    is to know there is light

    like a fox shrugging the flame in its fur
the rush of the creek after a summer storm

the whisper of wings as an owl haunts by
    a nest of bones where daffodils peek

    sap surging upwards to green and then leaf
branches that creak through the wind's endless sigh

though shadows may shift and re-shape their forms
    let the wedge of the moon act as a lure

    cast off the rooms where we've boxed ourselves tight
step into the den of the forest's deep heart

Marjorie Moorhead

Moon, Deer, Mountains, Stars

curtain time

When moon masquerades
as a whisp of cloud…
hiding in plain sight, shying
from earth's troubled faces, avoiding
that walker below, whose eyes pry, searching
heights for escape…or signs of hope

and a young deer appears at sidewalk edge
—gazes lock; walker, deer—frozen in a moment
of recognition. A flick of white as, in flight,
cloven tracks disappear into a scrim of nearby trees;
whose leaves flutter with a sigh of release.

Walk and walk now, upright one, until
skies purple with dusk, mountains blue
on distant horizon; vessels afloat in darkening tide.
Stars line up for tonight's debut…set to twinkle,
sparkling silver, like pin heads pushed into black,
as soon as night's curtain rises

Linda Laino

Firefly

i hooked your
light little firefly

like the tail of a thought.
it blazed through me carrying

a last chance like a
lottery ticket

and made a home
just long enough to

draw a map in a
lost woman my

useless brilliant body
without a lid to the jar

Simona Carini

Carson Pass

On the trail, slanted sun rays
marble rocks with shadows, night's
coolness inhabits the alpine forest.
Snow covers the ground in patches
melting into rivulets.

A dead Sierra juniper stretches out sun-washed,
twisted branches. It will fall and fall apart into
soil supporting seedlings and flowers.
In the company of a dead tree, my fear of dying
dwindles to a small knot loosened by a deep
breath of pine resin-perfumed air.

The trail ahead is lined with wildflowers:
red Indian paintbrush, purple lupine, white
phlox, yellow mule's ears. Above, the bold
blue of a clear summer sky—absolute,
like love.

I jump over running water, hear a rustling nearby:
a cinnamon-colored black bear waddles away.
The moment leaves before I am fully
aware of it. It will be a sweet
aftertaste—of sharp air, sunlight scattering
and a bear's breakfast interrupted.

When a snow patch extends beyond my line
of sight, I turn around. Frog Lake appears,
sapphire ruffled by a breeze.
On the shore, I unpack worries about work,
deadlines, a mammogram's date coming due.
I kneel down, drop them and let them float
away.

Devon Balwit

Winter Landscape with Bird Trap

It's the scale that awakens such tenderness
in us, Breughel's tiny doll babies

in their vast landscapes, each figure busy
like a flea

in a flea circus, caught by the leg. To us,
they are no different

than the songbirds approaching
the backyard trap,

seduced by life's fatness, the amassed harvest,
turning dainty circles

until they brush against time,
and it flattens them.

Brooke Harris

Flying West

Blinding snow. The wheels
don't touch the ground anymore,
they lurch with a mechanical grunt
to curl up to the plane's belly,
long talons of an eagle.

Darkness – blue black
with white diagonal lines
of sleet cloak the sky.
Pollock painting splattered
on the plexiglass window,
Rorschach inkblots smudged
in the clouds. Was that a moth
or a cat? A rabbit diving under
a fence? My chest thumps
with the immeasurable vastness sailing
two inches from my nose.

Through the clouds we climb
voiceless – floating on a blanket
of vapor. The sun's golden chain
skims the sky, a beacon calling
us from winter.

K.B. Ballentine

Crowding Out the Light

Rain again, but roses still bud
blood-red against another gray day.
Clover beckons, white-tongued petals
licking the air even as bees hum,
nuzzle into kiss-colored centers.

Two years ago drought browned
the mountains, burned patches on ridges
where pine once shaded laurel and fern.
The woods smoked for weeks –
a reminder of the searing sun, if we needed one.

The finch fashioned her nest by the front door again.
Every year she scolds us for leaving,
for returning, her small shelter tucked behind
a wreath of lavender. When she startles
from her eggs, I apologize, an urge
to stop, to peer into that woven darkness.

I want to sink into what's left
of that protective warmth. To remind myself
the smallest hearts can beat in fear.

Simona Carini

Life on the Edge

On the windblown bluff
splashed by salt spray
a tuft of Indian paintbrush—flames
of scarlet bracts—turned
the hostile slope into host.
Kelp-flavored air
in my lungs, I bloom here too.

Jari Chevalier

This Time of Year

Peacocks and peahens peck & strut.
In the lane the sun comes on full
& a heavy feather-bundle dragging behind
in dust & stones lifts, spreads. Behold
a libidinous pleasure as he lobs & twitches
its weight from the flared beds of quills.

In the evening, he climbs a huge pine
to the highest; his head ornament
springs like a jester's baubles, his luxuriant gown
trails elegant in air. Look at him — dream? Act?
Fantasm? Fact? When he opens his
throat the valley is shattered;
when he opens his eyes
the valley's intact.

Travis Stephens

Geese in Fields

There is little mystery
in the dark cold of late
December.
Even in California
cold rises from the earth.
Three days of rain have
encamped for the mountains.
There is a hope
of sunshine tomorrow
longer days ahead
and patience
always patience.
Geese have landed
in pools within fields
to snap at left grain like
misers set loose in a vault.
Vees of others pass over,
exchange insults or pleasantries
or both while a footsore
young coyote measures
the growing shore.
This is an artificial lake;
it will not last through summer.
Her hunger, though, is real.
The errant breeze regales
her with the scent of geese,
tadpole and distance between.

Sky breaks open,
a cloud grazes, ambles on…
In the pasture of sky
from Sonoma Mountain

to the headlands
a roundup has begun.
No branding irons needed
no horses to ride
just watch
the cloud hands gather
tally, corral grey mares.
They mill,
flick tails in annoyance.

Restless, dangerous
contained.
All is on pause,
the rain falling
and more to come.
Roots break from the
mud to catch a breath.
An egret stands at the edge,
patient, poking
into the blanket silence
so easily broken.

Roger Pfingston

Sandhill Cranes

It's their talk, barely heard,
that stops me–my tracks
etched in yesterday's snow–
craning to spot the migratory
flock, a burbling mass
hovering thousands of feet
in a sky so vastly bright
and blue it's hard to see
the slow turn of their
correction, a few like
threads tearing loose
before sewing themselves
back in place, their course
straight and true as I
continue, my direction
more notion than instinct,
my old neck hurting now,
remembering how my dad
at 86 passed out once,
looking up at something
he thought worth it
at the time.

Rebecca Dettorre

Encounter

A day for woods tramping, logs lifted
to reveal snakes, hornet nest and beehives
admired, sifting sandy soil below upended trees
to search for chert arrowheads.

Early spring, thin long sleeves, the sun a warm crown
as we looked up at woodpeckers and flawless sky.
Afternoon, we chose a place to eat and rest,
leaning in to our silence.

Headlong she ran, stopping a few feet before our knees,
placid eyes, softly mottled, heedless, curious.
We faced this guest, the breeze
tumbling live oak leaves.

It brought our scent of light sweat, taste
of fruit in mouth and air, to her. We took
each other in; she turned her neck, then
followed the herd's soundless admonition.

We were her first, the stillness
honored between us.

Cynthia Anderson

Arrival

here is the light
that allows another
day to happen

every living thing
leans toward that beam
from the east

golden after
the grey of dawn
a slight breeze

stirring branches
and leaves—
this is what

we came for
the light riding
higher

lengthening
shadows
behind us

. . . the clear
blue Barbicide air of this Americana

—Jennifer Hambrick, "Cut"

George Franklin

Noise of the World

In the kitchen, the refrigerator fan
Spins softly. Even piles of books
And papers on the dining room
Table seem to be resting. This is
The definition of solitude, the
House that quiet, the dog outside poking
His nose into opossum smells or
The pleasure of rotting leaves. In
The next room, my son is sleeping
Late, as he likes to do. I was the same
Way once. Now, I can't help waking
Early. I make myself coffee and
Eat leftover pita bread with honey.

The news is full of shouting, but
I'm reading it, not listening or
Watching reporters with perfect hair
Try to convey intensity. They're
Right, of course. The news is as bad
As it's ever been, but today something
Feels different. Above the back fence,
The trees are barely moving. They
Listen, in the way trees listen, to the sap
That moves beneath their bark. The
November air has spoken to them
Without words. Their lifespans are
Long; they don't anticipate illness
Or someone with a chainsaw cutting
Them down in pieces—the branches
First, then the trunk. "Future" is
A word too large for comprehension.

We say: "he never saw it coming" and
Feel wiser than whoever didn't see.
The opossums who live under the
Toolshed, though, and the quick rats who
Nest in the palm trees don't divide
Their lives that way, don't sit in the
Morning thinking about history, news,
Politics, about how arbitrarily we
Separate what happened yesterday from
The day before, and how the future always
Ends in chainsaws. But, we're not opossums
Or rats. History is the space we inhabit in
The meantime, the sounds of traffic that
Reach us when the back door is open,
Stories of people who've run out of
Choices, who've become part of the news.

That cup of coffee and the soft, white bread
Depend on being born here, not there. Then,
Not some other time. The refrigerator's
Fan grows louder. An airplane passes
Over the house on its way somewhere
West of here. The dog doesn't even look up.
The tree limbs don't move either. I want
To say this is what matters: solitude, the
Silence of trees and opossums, but it's
Not that easy. The noise of the world
Is always there, even when it's quiet.

*

When I wrote this last fall, no one
Was dying in my neighborhood except from
Clogged arteries or the occasional cancer.
A few months later, even the light has changed.
Afternoon sun burns through the window
The way kids set ants on fire with a magnifying
Glass, not quite believing their own power.

Today, the streets are quiet everywhere. In
New York, they're burying the dead in mass
Graves, and in Miami we don't know if we're
On the upside or downside of the curve.
Ximena and I wear masks and gloves to go
To the supermarket, lose count of how many
Times a day we've washed our hands. Last night,
There was no moon. We went for an illegal
Walk through a closed city park, its field
Vacant except for us and a few stars. We were
Afraid to sit on the benches and walked quickly.
There were no passing cars or planes to break
The silence, and we didn't speak.
The lights of the empty YMCA
Seemed possessed of a terrible sadness.

Nels Hanson

Trains

Where did they go, those mile-long
freight trains of childhood on tracks
cutting the dusty farm town in half, half
white, half brown, rich, poor, each hobo
king of his own flatcar, brave faces profiled
in wind from speed, blue from storybooks,
the young prince disowned and growing
older now on the dangerous journey to find
the princess. Box cars naked of graffiti
bore chalk numbers, letters only, strange
runes for routing cargoes somewhere
else and far where money waited to buy
their wares. Great Northern's proud rocky
mountain goat in silhouette upon its lone
peak, Union Pacific and Cotton Road
summoning Blue and Gray, Wabash
Cannonball with its song tipsy Dizzy Dean
crooned at seventh-inning stretch, B & O –
Baltimore and Ohio – that brought a smile,
Santa Fe, Rock Island Line's stone citadel
washed by ocean waves, Rio Grande crossing
the wide muddy river as years later Grateful
Dead would sing . . . Trains never stopped
but passed at 60 in a blur. When red lights
quit flashing there is only the red caboose
disappearing with its red beacon a backward
headlight as your father's pickup lurches
across raised iron rails like arms that surely
in some faint distance well beyond your
sight finally meet at their destination.

Marc Swan

The Yellow Wheelbarrow

for Dd

At the end of the lawn
where the steep slope falls
into the tributary that flows
in the spring melt,
years of accumulated debris
crowds the riverbank.
She parks the yellow wheelbarrow
with the flat-free tire,
carries her rake and shovel,
sometimes a pitchfork and loppers
to work the overgrown terrain
finding lost bottles, unbroken
ceramic and glass cups, metal plates,
a busted Zippo lighter,
and a pipe with a wooden bowl,
small animal skulls and bones,
tarnished silverware,
old tires and rims, rubber tubing,
ropes twisted and shredded,
thick metal pipes and drains,
yesterday a Victor Bo'Sun knife
rusted, but not beyond repair.
Treasures she uncovers
and spends hours cleaning
and polishing, removing years
of discarded disuse.
My concern is the slip and slide
of the tangled roots, wet leaves,
and grasses on the downside.
Today she took a whistle

to alert me if she falls.
In my office I hear a faint
call then more distinct
coming from the riverbank.
I rush to the door—
a cedar waxwing flies by.

Devon Balwit

Repeatedly
—*after Alberto Burri, Bianco cretto, 1973*

Both cloud and crust, I incarnate
ground zero for each megaton, the best

my brethren can bang out in factories.
Somewhere in a bunker, a soldier

under orders gets a bead on me and
depresses the trigger. I'm easy to hit

and know the drill. For a while, I am
nothing but shadow on brick, a Geiger-

counter sputter. After an eternity
of half-lives, I am once again habitable.

There is beauty in repeated shattering,
the kiln-glaze crackle of frantic lace.

Marc Swan

A Natural Voice

An older man in a red and green flannel shirt,
wire frame glasses, well-worn jeans,
wearing a blue Dodger's cap
sits a couple of stools from me.
He's on his third Bud since I've been here.
I'm nursing a second house chardonnay.
Glendale Boulevard dances in a stream
of light through narrow window panes.
I've been telling Maria behind the bar
about my year in Lake Tahoe.
The man turns to me with a quizzical look—
What do quaking aspens sound like?
I take a long pull on my chardonnay,
think back on weekly treks over the pass,
think of a herd of deer barely visible
in morning dew settled on the grassy knoll
before cresting the hill on Highway 89
to Alpine Village on to Markleeville.
In the fall I'd slow for a grove of aspens
singing their melody, shimmering
with their last golden breaths.
Hope, I tell the man with the Bud in his hand,
and possibility.

Gary Glauber

The Calculating

A little hole-in-the wall of a place,
five stools at the counter
and a magazine and news rack.
Each day the regulars would convene,
pick up their reserved racing forms
and start their notations, curious systems
with circles and symbols and odds,
a sort of personal calculus,
based on hunches and odds,
weather, breeding, trainers,
and the wisdom of a seasoned jockey.
Lonergin would kid about luck,
Devito would chomp on an unlit cigar,
Direnzo would engage Leon, the owner,
in some shared memory or another.
My job was to feign indifference,
to assume invisibility while also refilling
a coffee cup, providing some cake,
perhaps hitting the fountain for
an occasional celebratory egg cream.
I never knew anything more about them,
whether they had jobs, families, wives, children.
They in turn never asked anything more
than "Hey, how're y' doing?"
because it was never about me, but rather
about this busy place of temporary privacy,
a solidly packed tiny retail space
affording them the unlikely illusion
of infinite area, a place for contemplation
attentive to their needs, yet never nosy
enough to question their trifecta pick
on the fourth race that day at Aqueduct.

Steve Klepetar

What We Say to Ourselves

It's hard enough, with our brains on fire,
our hands empty, our blurry eyes strained.
We sit on the hard floor.
We pay attention to the wind.
We say to ourselves "this is my body, my breath."
We say to ourselves "this isn't pain, this is time passing."
With one eye closed, we see nothing.
One foot has fallen asleep, one ear has gone deaf.
We say to ourselves "we are learning what we can do without."
We say to ourselves "there is value in the grit, in the sand."
Across town the immigrants have arrived.
They are resting in the park with their sacks piled up in the
grass.
They are waiting by the church door.
Their children are sleeping a little while they can.
We say to ourselves "they are quiet and calm in their pain."
We say to ourselves "they will rest awhile and move on."

Susan Richardson

Lentils

There is a third world city down the street
and worlds away from my apartment.
I lurk inside the spaces between
shadows, listening to violence
explode in angry rhymes,
a figure eight of loathing that
skulks over scars in the pavement.
Next door lives beauty,
radiant in baggy briefs and
carrying a sawed off shot gun.
There is a man upstairs beating his wife.
A woman below throws
kitchen appliances at her girlfriend.
I am alone in a makeshift kitchen
slowly stirring lentils and
longing for the soothing
taste of silence.

Kari Gunter-Seymour

Badasses

Sunday afternoon. Taylor Swift's latest nonsense
caterwauls the radio, a third-string agitation,
compared to my son trying to bootlick his daughter
into jumping in our pond off the high dive,
nine feet up a steep planked ladder.

A pinch of a girl, she just this week turned six
and I wonder where that rascal in him comes from.
I blame his father, long gone and good riddance.
My true husband, a gem, who knows me all too well,
taps his sandaled foot against my pinky-toe,
slightly shakes his head, because my granddaughter
just cold-shouldered her daddy, ran to fetch
her fishing pole instead.

Though I don't want it, those twelve soccer boys,
clear the other side of the world, are on my mind.
Trapped miles inside a cave, tides rising, huddled
and hungry, licking water drops from crusty walls.
Last week, Navy SEALs rose from the depths
like apparitions, brought pep talks, promises,
concocting on the fly, ways those boys, who don't
even know how to swim, can strap on a face mask,
practice a few strokes, MacGyver their way free.

We cool ourselves in the water, ride four-wheelers,
reach for icy Coca-Colas, popsicles, slices of melon.
We're fixing to wind down when breaking
news grabs the radio. *Christ almighty*
four of those boys made it out, others
not far behind, SEALs at their backs, urging.

Soon after, my wily son afloat below the dive,
that plucky grandbaby of mine sets down her pole,
climbs the ladder, leaps like a fish-nymph,
hoots as she breaks the surface.

Patrick Theron Erickson

Behold, I Stand at the Door and Knock

needs a door
and a door knocker
like old homes have

perhaps of brass
or wrought iron

and the brass tarnished
and the wrought iron rusted
from so many sweaty fingers

needs one who knocks
just outside the door

and one who opens
just inside

with only the door
and the threshold between them

whether the door is open
or closed

An open and shut affair
needs rewording

lest the one who knocks
and the one who opens
be misunderstood

I read of a culture
where only the thief knocks
to see if anyone is home

Friends and visitors
do not knock
but signal their coming
in a shrill greeting
some way off

a harangue
which needs no rewording

lest the knocker
be misinformed

and the one just inside the door
mistaken

with the door and the threshold
between them

and both be wary
and both beware.

Revelation 3:20

Alan Catlin

Watching the Chernobyl Explosion and Subsequent Fires like Whistler's Nocturne in Blue and Gold: Fireworks Falling

They witnessed history that night,
those dead people watching on the
footbridge of imminent death.
All of them watched the disaster
happening, one that was years in
the making: all those corners cut, rules
ignored, unrealistic parameters set,
leading here, to the inevitable, the worst
possible outcome. All those people
unaware, not warned of consequences,
none of them suspecting watching was
a curiosity that kills, that night the
unnatural fires burned the skin off
the night, shooting geysers of light
no one could turn away from even if
they knew it was already too late.
While the adults watched, children
played in radioactive dust, shredded
death notes that fell like wayward out-of-
season snow, each more toxic than the last
one and the next. All of them transfixed
by this fireworks display, the grand finale
of a light show that would define the age,
turn their skin to jelly, their retinas to
melting wax, all of them victims
of an unforgiving power play, one
whose half-life is fifty millennia long.

John Palen

Smooth Dark Seed

The window silences the wind
that tosses bare maples
and needle-laden pines.
They bow to the wind,
spring back
and bow again.

In the next room
a cellist practices
a musical phrase,
only a few notes
that she repeats
again and again,

centering and shaping
until the house fills
with smooth dark seed
with winter coming on.

Alan Catlin

Detainee Refugee Camp, USA

He looks as if he were born
to spend his life in a yard surrounded
by fifteen foot high concrete walls,
topped with rolls of barbed wires,
and buttressed by guard towers.
He looks like Harry Houdini on
a five day drunk waking up on
Riker's Island, freshly tattooed
with iguanas on each arm and death
head skulls on each side of his chest.
"Mia madre con amor" it says, in script,
between the talking heads and the devil
looking up from his navel as if amused,
holding a trident that pokes the hull
of a ship whose mast and crew have
seen better days and much troubled water.
The man whose body contains all this woe,
bears an expression that suggests:
I can break these bonds, I can slip
free from these handcuffs, I can,
if only I knew how.

Kersten Christianson

Conscience

I am that raven
shadow *klaw-*
klawking over
your shoulder,

that dried tea
bag in an empty
mug, cool
to the touch.

That itch
to walk on two
strong legs
in speakeasy sun,

the *whoosh*
and *swish* of baby
waves on high
tide gravel.

I am your *maybe,*
what if, what if I
don't.

Lachlan Brooks

God Moves In

Mysterious ways; mystery man, manly macho man,
mimicry man and mime and moaning, drowning man,
and flood man, mimetic man, mountains and molehills man,
a man for all seasons, ice man, man-made, motionless man;
God moves in, because he burst his seams, muddy man,
a man of action, man of many faces, faceless man,
facetious man, man of myth and motion, man of thorns,
man of cuckoldry and bestiality, man of horns,
of sea and seasickness and sickly complexions;
The god complex: god is complex, and it turns out
(mysterious ways) god moves in next door
and he's a difficult neighbor-man, man-made man,
moot man, old-fashioned out-of-date and out of print man,
man of loose morals, immoral man, morality man and
monetary man, useless man, man with no hands man,
washed up man, rules and regulations and demands man,
sin and mercy man, man in a box, cardboard cut-out man,
permission man and attrition man, running out of ideas man,
gout and grout and grumbling man, cardboard man,
get-into-a-box man, easily boxed up, retractable man,
packable man, past his sell-by date man, token man,
moving in next door, little patched-up broken man,
man of letters, man of chance, the drop of a dime man,
stuck in the past man, knows-he's-past-his-prime man;
gods move in every day, man, men and mirthlessness,
mundane neighbors, now, men of god and godlessness;
leave me be, gods, odds are and odds are not, gods,
and if you let me be, you gods or men next door, odds
are that I'll let you be, be you gods or men or frauds.

Jennifer Hambrick

Cut

It seems birdsong is outdated,
that I can't bathe in it or drink It.
And they tell me that we're over

cicada song, too, and that I'm not
allowed to wrap it around my husband's
shoulders. That means the sun rising

as day begins is so last century, and
watching moonlight sparkle on a river
is what all the old guys talk about

at the barber shop, and the barber steers
the chatter just like he used to hairpin
turn that red Chevelle at night on narrow

dirt roads between his parents' house
and hers, knowing that the stars
wouldn't give away their secrets.

Whatever stories on an average day
well up in hackneyed hearts and stumble
out as platitudes, mixing with the clear

blue Barbicide air of this Americana
scene from Central Casting, its pole
twisting red-white-blue outside

with the trite laziness of summer,
and the barber inside shaping necklines,
snipping gray away from temples,

taking a little off the top down
to the pompadour held in place so firm
and deep inside each one of them.

Jeff Burt

Written On Walt Whitman's Birthday

Down on the ancient wharf, the sand, I sit, with a new-comer chatting
—Walt Whitman, "Twenty Years"

I finish the long walk to the Santa Cruz wharf
where grace pervades on a bench
when the sun burns off the fog
with Whitman chatting in my ears,
hear his tones on the wood and steel
in thrums of arrhythmic leather,
soles of rubber squeaking like clarinets,
and I think he'd like the collar-less throng
in tennis shoes and cheap sandals,
uncoordinated jazzy high-pitch roast of leisure
among the regular grind of work,
how he'd listen to my life and pull me from the wind
like an anonymous tuft and weave me into the fabric
of a nation, turn anomie into bonhomie,
how, with head bent down from the enormous weight
of inclusive thought, he'd exalt the beautiful
ugliness of toes, long for warm bowls of water,
soapsuds, and a thousand hands rubbing feet.

Ace Boggess

If I Came in Here Shot, Would You Say I Had a Lead Problem?
—John Van Kirk, *Song for Chance*

I'd say you had an America problem—
wrong place, wrong situation.

I'd say you could use a good drug problem
or never-ending cup of whiskey,
good stuff first, cheapest ever after.

I'd say you've sprung a leak,
might need a cork, or rubber cement.

I'd say I can't stand the sight of blood,
the site of blood, the cited blood.

I'd say *have a seat, friend,*
while we wait for the wound to pass—

as if any of our pretty eruptions
leave the petty party memory is.

Don't know bullet holes, but
I have punctured & been jabbed.
I've walked face-first into a fist.

Who hasn't had his nostril opened
like a box-wine tap; eye
purpled, yellowed in the healing;
tasted rust-mouth or the salty underlip?

Don't come in here shot if you can help it.
If you can't, I'd say you had

a weakness where stability should be,
especially at your age, even at mine.

I'd say you had an insurance problem.
I'd offer to pick up the check,
but it's not my turn.

George Franklin

Crivelli's Madonna and Child

The world is just as beautiful as it's hurt.
A fly's landed next to the child, the stone is cracked.
Poised on a cushion and yellow cloth, alert,
Bird clutched to heart, he observes but doesn't act.

A fly's landed next to the child, the stone is cracked,
A knobby gourd, ripe apples shade the skies.
Bird clutched to heart, he observes but doesn't act.
The world is broken marble; we are flies.

A knobby gourd, ripe apples shade the skies,
Mauve silk and branches held by nothing seen.
The world is broken marble; we are flies.
Behind him is the orchard's endless green.

Mauve silk and branches held by nothing seen,
Poised on a cushion and yellow cloth, alert,
Behind him is the orchard's endless green.
The world is just as beautiful as it's hurt.

Peter Leight

The Other Day We Were Standing Around in the Wings

waiting to take our seats in the back where we sit when we're not
in the front and on the side when we're not in the middle, trying
to feel friendly, applauding on occasion, flapping our hands like
rudimentary wings, not even noticing the faith or creed of those
around us, which is often weakly opportunistic, not even
thinking about the race or ethnicity that reflects the geographical
origins of their ancestors, waiting for them to come from where
they are, which is always interesting when it happens, not even
concerning ourselves with the gender identity that often
determines how people feel or how they think about the feelings
opening up in them like wings, much less the sexual orientation,
which is also related to love because our feelings about
ourselves are so closely tied to our feelings about each other the
way a wing touches the air on both sides.

Mercedes Lawry

Heartstrings

If I had stayed with the banjo girl, I might still be whole.
That girl playing on her tilted porch taught me
everything about sorrow. I knew the backbone
and inside the mouth and all the soft places
between toes. The birds came around more easily,
whatever the sky's blush. I could be trusted there,
not to take things lightly, not to betray
my old darlings or those gathered around for scraps.
Her voice could take you straight down
into a grave and back out again.
She could lay beside you on the soft moss
by the creek and make nothing at all an effort.

There's not too many voices that can tear
your heart into thin strips and put them back
without showing a seam. I'm swallowed
by neon now and there's not a simple truth in sight.
I'm an off-key old fool, growing crooked and tired
in a too-late version of my life, a sorry, sour note
with nothing left except amens.

Martin Willitts, Jr.

Endings

In the poor light of late evening,
remembrance goes out.

Let it. Every day has an ending:
a lifetime of stars filling the sky.

Nightjars graze what remains of today,
making chinks in our heart.

Allow this day to end
with its needles of light piercing the dark.

Let multitudes of singing fill the end.
Let exaltations of the soul leap out.

Louisa Muniz

I Ask God To Turn Up The Volume
Upon Hearing the News of Pittsburgh

God, why have you grown so silent?

In prayer I bloodlet sadness
splintered thin   on wooden floors.

Time stands still. Demons root
in the marrow of living.

To blow-soften daily news   I wear
rose-colored glasses & cordless ear plugs.

Help me understand.   Lift me
from darkness to alpenglow.

Turn up the volume. Say
what you have to say. The quiet nails

my throat. Even the trees are growing ears
in the netted veins of their leaves.

Daily, I sweeten bread in blessings
& on good days I still find you

in cherry blossoms   a bolt
of riotous bloom

swelling apricot skies   & plaiting
patterns in sunlit branches

When they say,
It's a terrible day for this country,

Don't you think   we love hard enough?

Ace Boggess

Hair Metal

We didn't call it that
until after we put aside
guitars & dreams
of a colorful existence.

A kind of music broke inside us,
silenced by the 90s,
loss of hope of happiness.

We had fun pretending
before Cobain stopped,
before the President
said, "I feel your pain,"

& like him, we wanted to scream
we were still relevant.

Joyful, wasn't it? Its gospel
didn't require we care
about anything.

John Leonard

Something Stays Behind

How long was this day? How vacant were the pills?
A kiss that tasted like iron, the electric scent of sawdust,
cold lips pressed against the glass; a feeling you could only
describe as *sky*. Or maybe it was a deer fighting the forest—
cheek to cheek, musk on bark for miles—only to end as blood
stained on asphalt, fur reflected on chrome. When drowning
becomes a reflex, becomes an empty field of open eyes at dusk.
When the last contrail folds into itself and becomes endless night.
And when it's only us, what comes after dying?
What comes after all this time hiding from the light?

Jeff Burt

Purity

I wasn't good at listening, my mother said,
though I could hear just fine,
because listening meant obeying,
and other times it meant understanding in the moment
and then obeying tomorrow or whenever
that moment came again, or listening meant
a revelation could occur if I was quiet
and sitting still, like waiting for the crush
of a hoof on a leaf and then seeing a deer
poke its nose out of the arbor.

Truth was like that sometimes, she said,
not like a math equation where it solves
all kinds of problems, or a science discovery
that cures or changes how we are with things,
not the pulpits shall and shall nots,
but like Dr. King when his voice pierced the rain
from underneath his umbrella
and a glimpse of sunshine came from his words,
or listening to the way Rudy Schwartz sang
head bent over left with a wide-open mouth
and his shoes bent from tippy-toes.

When you listen, you'll think of purity, she said,
of the clear cold water of the artesian spring
by the creek by the mill
just after it crosses under the highway
on the south side of the hill on a warm day.

CONTRIBUTORS

Cynthia Anderson has published eleven poetry collections, most recently *Full Circle* (Cholla Needles, 2022). Her poems appear frequently in journals and anthologies, and she is a Pushcart Prize and Best of the Net nominee. She makes her home in the Mojave Desert near Joshua Tree National Park.

K.B. Ballentine' seventh poetry collection, *Edge of Echo*, was published by Iris Press. Her earlier books can be found with Blue Light Press, Middle Creek Publishing, and Celtic Cat Publishing. Published in *North Dakota Quarterly, Atlanta Review* and *Haight-Ashbury Literary Journal*, as well as in numerous anthologies

Devon Balwit's poems and reviews can be found in *The Worcester Review, The Cincinnati Review, Tampa Review, Barrow Street, Rattle* and *Grist* among others. Her most recent collections are *Rubbing Shoulders with the Greats* (Seven Kitchens Press 2020) and *Dog-Walking in the Shadow of Pyongyang* (Nixes Mate Books, 2021).

Gary Beaumier is the author of two books of poetry *From My Family to Yours* published through Finishing Line Press and *Dented Brown Fedora* published by Uncollected Press. He has been a boat builder, a teacher, a garbage man, a bookstore manager and a Gandy dancer amongst many other occupations. He once taught poetry in a women's prison.

Stephen Black is a poet and narrative writer who lives in Gibson County, Tennessee, with his Walker Coonhound, Henry D. His work explores ecology, culture, natural history, bioregionalism, and the often tense relationships between people and the places they inhabit. He is currently working on a landscape memoir in verse.

Ace Boggess is author of six books of poetry, most recently *Escape Envy* (Brick Road Poetry Press, 2021). His writing has appeared in *Michigan Quarterly Review, Notre Dame Review, Harvard Review,* and other journals. An ex-con, he lives in Charleston, West Virginia, where he writes and tries to stay out of trouble.

Carl Boon is the author of the full-length collection *Places & Names: Poems* (The Nasiona Press, 2019). His writing has appeared in many journals and magazines, including *Prairie Schooner, Posit,* and *The Maine Review*. He currently lives in Izmir, Turkey, where he teaches American literature at Dokuz Eylül University.

Rebecca Brock is a graduate of the Bennington Writing Seminars. She was a finalist in the 2021 Joy Harjo Poetry Contest. Idaho born, she is raising her two sons in Virginia and still isn't used to the humidity. Her first chapbook will be available Fall 2022 from Kelsay Books. You can find more of her work at rebeccabrock.org.

Lachlan Brooks is a New York-based writer and actor. She holds an MA from Columbia University and a BFA from NYU's Tisch School of the Arts. Her poetry has appeared in publications including *Poet Lore*, *The Decadent Review*, *The Remembered Arts Journal*, the *Chronogram* magazine, and *The Year: A Crack the Spine Anthology: 2019*.

Kathleen S. Burgess is a former Ohio Poetry Association vice-president who has juried and toured with Women of Appalachia's Women Speak. Senior editor at *Pudding Magazine* and assistant editor at *Northern Appalachia Review*, she's received four Pushcart and two Best of the Net nominations. Among five poetry collections are *What Burdens Do Those Trains Bear Away* (Bottom Dog Press, 2018) and *The Wonder Cupboard* (NightBallet Press, 2019). She is a retired public school music teacher living with her husband just outside Chillicothe, Ohio.

Jeff Burt lives in Santa Cruz County, California, with his wife and a July abundance of plums He has also contributed to *Heartwood, Williwaw Journal, Red Wolf Journal,* and *Rat's Ass Review*. He won the Cold Mountain Review 2017 Poetry Prize.

Simona Carini was born in Perugia, Italy. She writes poetry and nonfiction and has been published in various venues, in print and online. She lives in Northern California with her husband and works as a data scientist at an academic research institution. Her first collection *Surival Time* is available from Sheila-Na-Gig Editions.

Alan Catlin has been publishing since the seventies. Among his many chapbooks are a noir series of movie poems collected in award winning chapbook, *Blue Velvet* (Slipstream), the chapbook *Hollyweird* (Night Ballet Press), and three full-length books of three chapbooks each: *Lessons in Darkness* (Luchador Press), *The Road to Perdition* (Alien Buddha) and forthcoming, *Exterminating Angels* (Kelsay Books).

Jari Chevalier's poems have appeared in *Beloit Poetry Journal, Boulevard, The Cincinnati Review, Green Mountains Review, Gulf Coast Online, The Massachusetts Review, Ploughshares,* and other journals. She holds an MA in Creative Writing from CCNY and a BA cum laude in Literature and Writing from Columbia University.

Kersten Christianson is a poet and English teacher from Sitka, Alaska. She is the author of *Curating the House of Nostalgia* (Sheila-Na-Gig, 2020), *What Caught Raven's Eye* (Petroglyph Press, 2018), and *Something Yet to Be Named* (Kelsay Books, 2017). She is also the poetry editor for *Alaska Women Speak*. Kersten enjoys road trips, bookstores, and smooth ink pens.

Sandy Coomer is a poet, artist, Ironman athlete, and social entrepreneur from Nashville, TN. She is the author of 3 poetry chapbooks and 2 full-length collections, *Available Light* (Iris Press, 2019), and *The Broken Places* (Saddle Road Press, 2021). She is the editor of the online journal *Rockvale Review* and the director of Rockvale Writers' Colony. Her favorite word is "believe."

Joe Cottonwood is a home improvement contractor. He lives under redwood trees in the Santa Cruz Mountains of California raising curly-haired dogs and straight-haired grandchildren while dodging wildfires and the occasional lion. His most recent book of poetry is *Random Saints*.

Rebecca Dettorre has lived in Ohio, West Virginia, Kentucky, Florida, Tennessee. Nostalgia is her curse and blessing, bringing her home.

William Doreski lives in Peterborough, New Hampshire. His most recent book of poetry is *Mist in Their Eyes* (2021). He has published three critical studies, including *Robert Lowell's Shifting Colors*. His essays, poetry, fiction, and reviews have appeared in many journals.

Patrick Theron Erickson, a resident of Garland, Texas, a Tree City, just south of Duck Creek, is a retired parish pastor put out to pasture himself. Besides a chapbook, *Better Late Than Never* (The Orchard Street Press, 2022), his work has appeared in *Sheila-Na-Gig online, Tipton Poetry Journal,* and *Grey Sparrow Journal,* among other publications.

Michael Estabrook has been publishing his poetry in the small press since the 1980s. He has published over 20 collections, a recent one being *The Poet's Curse, A Miscellany* (The Poetry Box, 2019). He lives in Acton, Massachusetts.

George Franklin's collections include *Noise of the World, Travels of the Angel of Sorrow, Among the Ruins / Entre las ruinas,* and *Traveling for No Good Reason. Remote Cities,* his newest book, is on the way from Sheila-Na-Gig Editions. He practices law in Miami and teaches in Florida prisons.

Matthew James Friday is a British born writer and teacher now based in Oregon. He has been published in numerous international journals, including: *Dawntreader* (UK), *The Dillydoun Review* (USA), and *Lunch Ticket* (USA). He has had micro-chapbooks published by the Origami Poems Project (USA). Matthew is a 2021 Pushcart Prize nominated poet.

Gary Glauber is a widely published poet, fiction writer, teacher, and former music journalist. His fifth full-length collection is Inside Outrage (Sheila-Na-Gig Editions). He also has authored two chapbooks, *Memory Marries Desire* (Finishing Line Press) and *The Covalence of Equanimity* (SurVision Books), a winner of the 2019 James Tate International Poetry Prize.

Carol Lynn Stevenson Grellas is a recent graduate of Vermont College of Fine Arts, MFA in Writing program. She's an eleven-time Pushcart Prize nominee and a seven-time Best of the Net nominee. Her latest collection of poems *Alice in Ruby Slippers* was short-listed for the 2021 Eric Hoffer Grand Prize book award.

John Grey is an Australian poet, US resident, recently published *in Sheepshead Review, Stand, Poetry Salzburg Review* and *Hollins Critic.* Latest books, *Leaves On Pages, Memory Outside The Head* and *Guest Of Myself* are available through Amazon. Work upcoming in *Ellipsis, Blueline* and *International Poetry Review.*

Kari Gunter-Seymour is the Poet Laureate of Ohio and a recipient of a 2021 Academy of American Poets Laureate Fellowship. Her poetry collection *A Place So Deep Inside America It Can't Be Seen* (Sheila-Na-Gig Editions), won the 2020 Ohio Poet of the Year Award. Her newest collection is *Alone in the House of My Heart* (Swallow Press, 2022).Her work has been featured on *Verse Daily, The New York Times, World Literature Today* and *Poem-a-Day.*

Jennifer Hambrick (Columbus, Ohio), four-time pushcart nominee, is the author of the Stevens Prize-winning *In the High Weeds, Joyride* (Red Moon Press) and *Unscathed* (NightBallet Press). Hambrick is featured in *American Life in Poetry*. She won the Sheila-Na-Gig Press Poetry Contest (Fall 2020), and many other awards. jenniferhambrick.com.

Nels Hanson has worked as a farmer, teacher and contract writer/editor. His fiction received the San Francisco Foundation's James D. Phelan Award and Pushcart nominations in 2010, 2012, 2014 and 2016. His poems received a 2014 Pushcart nomination, *Sharkpack Review's* 2014 Prospero Prize, and 2015 and 2016 Best of the Net nominations.

Alan Harris is a hospice volunteer who helps patients write memoirs, letters, and poetry. Harris is the recipient of the John Clare Poetry Prize as well as the Tompkins Poetry Award from Wayne State University. Harris is a three-time Pushcart nominee. His published collections include *Fall Ball* and *Hospice Bed Conversations*.

Brooke Harris is an artist and writer who calls Lexington, Kentucky home. With an MFA in Writing from Spalding University and her love for art, she creates poems and paintings that evoke memory and emotion. Brooke teaches painting and writing classes and also loves to explore new places.

Donna Hilbert's latest books are *Threnody*, Moon Tide Press, 2022, and *Gravity: New & Selected Poems*, Tebot Bach, 2018. She is a monthly contributor to the on-line journal *Verse-Virtual*. Work has been featured on podcasts *The Writer's Almanac, Lyric Life,* and *Writers on Writing.* She lives in Southern California.

Seth Jani lives in Seattle, WA and is the founder of Seven Circle Press. His work has appeared in *The American Poetry Journal*, *Chiron Review*, *Ghost City Review*, *Rust+Moth* and *Pretty Owl Poetry*, among others. His full-length collection, *Night Fable*, was published by FutureCycle Press in 2018.

Sean Kelbley lives on a southeastern Ohio farm. He works as a primary school counselor. In addition to *Sheila-Na-Gig online*, his poetry has appeared in *One, Rattle, Sugar House Review*, and other wonderful places, and has been nominated for Best of the Net, Best New Poets, and the Pushcart Prize.

Steve Klepetar lives in the Berkshires in Massachusetts. His fourteen poetry collections include *My Son Writes a Report on the Warsaw Ghetto, My Father Teaches Me a Magic Word, The Li Bo Poems,* and *A Landscape in Hell.*

Judy Kronenfeld's fifth collection of poetry, *Groaning and Singing*, was published by FutureCycle Press in February 2022. Previous collections include *Bird Flying through the Banquet* (FutureCycle, 2017) and *Shimmer* (WordTech, 2012). Her poems have appeared widely in journals including *Cider Press Review, MacQueen's Quinterly, New Ohio Review, Offcourse, Pratik, Siant,* and *Verdad.*

Linda Laino is an artist and writer with an MFA from Virginia Commonwealth University. She resides in San Miguel de Allende, Mexico where the surreal atmosphere and sensuous colors have wormed their way into her paintings. Finding beautiful things on the ground is a favorite pastime.

Mercedes Lawry is the author of three chapbooks, the latest, *In the Early Garden with Reason,*was selected by Molly Peacock for the 2018 WaterSedge Chapbook Contest. Her poetry has appeared in such journals as *Poetry, Nimrod,* and *Prairie Schooner* and has been nominated seven times for a Pushcart Prize .

Peter Leight lives in Amherst, Massachusetts. He has previously published poems in *Paris Review, AGNI, Antioch Review, Beloit Poetry Journal, FIELD, New World, Raritan,* and other magazines

John Leonard is an English teacher and poetry editor for *Twyckenham Notes*. He holds an M.A. in English from Indiana University. His previous works have appeared in *Chiron Review, december, Roanoke Review, North Dakota Quarterly, The Windsor Review,* and *Trailer Park Quarterly*. He lives in Elkhart, Indiana with his wife.

Tamara Madison is the author of the chapbook *The Belly Remembers* and two full-length volumes of poetry, *Wild Domestic* and *Moraine*. Her work has appeared in *Chiron Review, Your Daily Poem, the Writer's Almanac, Sheila-Na-Gig* and many other publications.

Betsy Mars is a poet, photographer, and an assistant editor at *Gyroscope Review*. Her poems have been nominated for the Best of the Net and Pushcart Prize. Betsy's photos have been featured in *RATTLE's Ekphrastic Challenge, Spank the Carp,* and *Redheaded Stepchild*. She is the author of two books, one co-authored with Alan Walowitz.

Jessica Mehta, PhD is a multi-award-winning Aniyunwiya (citizen of the Cherokee Nation) poet and artist. She is currently a Fulbright Nehru Senior Scholar and working on her 16th book.

Michael Minassian is a contributing editor for *Verse-Virtual*, an online poetry journal. His chapbooks include poetry: *The Arboriculturist* and photography: *Around the Bend*. His poetry collections *Time is Not a River, Morning Calm,* and *A Matter of Timing* are all available on Amazon.

Daniel Edward Moore lives in Washington on Whidbey Island. His poems are forthcoming in *Notre Dame Review, Front Range Review, Ocotillo Review, Iron Horse Literary Review, Steam Ticket Journal* and *The Meadow*. His recent book, *'Psalmania'* was a finalist for the Four Way Books Levis Prize in Poetry.

Marjorie Moorhead writes from the NH/VT border. She originally found her voice while examining a long and formative survival journey. Marjorie's poems are collected in two chapbooks, many anthologies, and literary journals. A full collection is forthcoming in Spring 2022.

Louisa Muniz lives in Sayreville, N.J. She holds a Master's in Curriculum and Instruction from Kean University. Her work has appeared in *Tinderbox Journal, Palette Poetry, PANK Magazine, Shark Reef* and elsewhere. She has been nominated for Best of the Net and a Pushcart Prize. Her chapbook, *After Heavy Rains* was released in 2020.

John Palen's *Riding With the Diaspora* won the Sheila-Na-Gig Poetry Chapbook Contest and was published in April. John has recent work appearing or forthcoming in *Spoon River Poetry Review, Cider Press Review,* and *Sleet.* He lives on the Illinois Grand Prairie

Roger Pfingston is a retired teacher of English and photography. He is the recipient of a poetry fellowship from the National Endowment for the Arts and two PEN Syndicated Fiction Awards. Roger is the author of five chapbooks, the most recent being *What's Given,* available from Kattywompus Press.

David B. Prather is the author of *We Were Birds*. His work has appeared in many journals, including Prairie Schooner, Colorado Review, Seneca Review, Still: The Journal, and many others. He studied acting at the National Shakespeare Conservatory, and he studied writing at Warren Wilson College.

Vivian Faith Prescott was born and raised in Tlingit Aaní in Wrangell, Ḵaachx̱ana.áak'w, a small island in Southeast Alaska, where she lives and writes at her family's fish camp. She's the author of several poetry collections, a book of linked stories, and a foodoir about life at her fish camp.

Phill Provance is the author of the poetry collection *A Plan in Case of Morning* and the chapbook *The Day the Sun Rolled Out of the Sky*, His poetry and prose have appeared in *The Baltimore Sun, The Cimarron Review, The Crab Creek Review, Cricket: Spider,* and many others. Among his honors are grants from Poets & Writers and PEN America.

Duncan Richardson's fiction, poetry and history have appeared in various magazines and books, including *Subtropical Suspense* and *Futurevisions*. He writes fulltime in Brisbane, Australia. His non-fiction work includes *Year of Disaster-Brisbane 1864, Captives of the Spanish Lady* and *Civilising Brisbane.*

Susan Richardson is an award winning, internationally published poet. She is the author of *Things My Mother Left Behind* from Potter's Grove Press, and also writes the blog, "Stories from the Edge of Blindness."

Stan Sanvel Rubin's poems have appeared in *Agni, Poetry Northwest, Georgia Review,* and others. His four full-length collections include *There. Here.* (Lost Horse Press) and *Hidden Sequel* (Barrow Street Book Prize). He lives on the north Olympic Peninsula of Washington state.

Dan Sicoli authored two poetry chapbooks from Pudding House, *Pagan Supper and the allegories.* He's published poems in numerous lit mags, anthologies, and electronic outlets. When not editing *Slipstream,* you might find him in a gin mill banging on an old Gibson with a garage rock band somewhere in Western New York State.

Travis Stephens is a tugboat captain who resides with his family in California. A University of Wisconsin-Eau Claire alumni, his book of poetry, *"skeeter bit & still drunk"* was published by Finishing Line Press in 2022.

Stuart Stromin is a South African-American writer and filmmaker, living in Los Angeles. He was educated at Rhodes University, South Africa, the Alliance Francaise de Paris, and UCLA. His work has been published by *Jalada Africa, Nzuri, The Chaffin Journal, Immigrant Report, Macabre Ladies, Dissident Voice, Sheila-na-gig online,* etc

Marc Swan, a retired vocational rehabilitation counselor, lives in coastal Maine. Poems recently published or forthcoming in *Gargoyle, Crannóg, Paterson Literary Review, Misfit, Queen's Quarterly,* among others. His fifth collection, *all it would take,* was published in 2020 by tall-lighthouse (UK).

Alan Walowitz is a Contributing Editor at *Verse-Virtual, an Online Community Journal of Poetry.* His chapbook, *Exactly Like Love,* comes from Osedax Press. The full-length, *The Story of the Milkman and Other Poems,* is available from Truth Serum Press. Most recently, from Arroyo Seco Press, is the chapbook *In the Muddle of the Night,* written with poet Betsy Mars.

Martin Willitts, Jr. edits the *Comstock Review.* His 25 chapbooks include the Turtle Island Quarterly Editor's Choice Award, *The Wire Fence Holding Back the World* (Flowstone Press, 2017), plus 21 full-length collections includes 2019 Blue Light Award *The Temporary World* and *All Wars Are the Same War* (FutureCycle Press, 2022).

Author Index

Sheila-Na-Gig Editions